Bilingual
VISUAL
dictionary

Bilingual
VISUAL
dictionary

Previously published as part of
5-Language Visual Dictionary

London, New York, Melbourne, Munich, Delhi

Senior Editor Angeles Gavira
Senior Art Editor Ina Stradins
DTP Designers Sunil Sharma, Balwant Singh,
Harish Aggarwal, John Goldsmid, Ashwani Tyagi
DTP Coordinator Pankaj Sharma
Production Controller Liz Cherry
Picture Researcher Anna Grapes
Managing Editor Liz Wheeler
Managing Art Editor Phil Ormerod
Category Publisher Jonathan Metcalf

Designed for Dorling Kindersley by WaltonCreative.com
Art Editor Colin Walton, assisted by Tracy Musson
Designers Peter Radcliffe, Earl Neish, Ann Cannings
Picture Research Marissa Keating

Language content for Dorling Kindersley by
g-and-w PUBLISHING
Managed by Jane Wightwick, assisted by Ana Bremón
Translation and editing by Christine Arthur
Additional input by Dr. Arturo Pretel, Martin Prill,
Frédéric Monteil, Meinrad Prill, Mari Bremón,
Oscar Bremón, Anunchi Bremón, Leila Gaafar

First American Edition, 2005
Published in the United States by
DK Publishing, Inc., 375 Hudson Street,
New York, New York 10014
20 19 18 17 16 15 14 13 12 11
040-BD221-Aug/05
Copyright © 2005 Dorling Kindersley Limited

All rights reserved under International and
Pan-American Copyright Conventions. No part of
this publication may be reproduced, stored in a
retrieval system, or transmitted in any form or by
any means, electronic, mechanical, photocopying,
recording or otherwise, without the prior written
permission of the copyright owner. Published in
Great Britain by Dorling Kindersley Limited.

A Cataloging-in-Publication record for this book
is available from the Library of Congress.
ISBN-13: 978-0-7566-1295-5

Color reproduction by Colourscan, Singapore
Printed and bound in China by L-Rex

Discover more at
www.dk.com

Inhalt
contents

die Gesundheit
health

auswärts essen
eating out

die Freizeit
leisure

deutsch • english

auswärts essen •
eating out

das Lernen • study

die Arbeit • work

der Verkehr •
transport

der Sport • sport

die Freizeit • leisure

die Umwelt •
environment

die Information •
reference

über das Wörterbuch

Bilder helfen erwiesenermaßen, Informationen zu verstehen und zu behalten. Dieses zweisprachige Wörterbuch enthält eine Fülle von Illustrationen und präsentiert gleichzeitig ein umfangreiches aktuelles Vokabular in zwei europäischen Sprachen.

Das Wörterbuch ist thematisch gegliedert und behandelt eingehend die meisten Bereiche des heutigen Alltags, vom Restaurant und Fitnesscenter, Heim und Arbeitsplatz bis zum Tierreich und Weltraum. Es enthält außerdem Wörter und Redewendungen, die für die Unterhaltung nützlich sind und das Vokabular erweitern.

Dies ist ein wichtiges Nachschlagewerk für jeden, der sich für Sprachen interessiert – es ist praktisch, anregend und leicht zu benutzen.

Einige Anmerkungen

Die zwei Sprachen werden immer in der gleichen Reihenfolge aufgeführt – Deutsch und Englisch.

Substantive werden mit den bestimmten Artikeln, die das Geschlecht (Maskulinum, Femininum oder Neutrum) und den Numerus (Singular oder Plural) ausdrücken, angegeben, zum Beispiel:

der Samen   **die Mandeln**
seed   almonds

Die Verben sind durch ein (v) nach dem englischen Wort gekennzeichnet:

ernten • harvest (v)

Am Ende des Buchs befinden sich Register für jede Sprache. Sie können dort ein Wort in einer der zwei Sprachen und die jeweilige Seitenzahl nachsehen.
Die Geschlechtsangabe erfolgt mit folgenden Abkürzungen:

m = Maskulinum
f = Femininum
n = Neutrum

about the dictionary

The use of pictures is proven to aid understanding and the retention of information. Working on this principle, this highly illustrated bilingual dictionary presents a large range of useful current vocabulary in two European languages.

The dictionary is divided thematically and covers most aspects of the everyday world in detail, from the restaurant to the gym, the home to the workplace, outer space to the animal kingdom. You will also find additional words and phrases for conversational use and for extending your vocabulary.

This is an essential reference tool for anyone interested in languages— practical, stimulating, and easy to use.

A few things to note

The two languages are always presented in the same order—German and English.

In German, nouns are given with their definite articles reflecting the gender (masculine, feminine or neuter) and number (singular or plural), for example:

der Samen   **die Mandeln**
seed   almonds

Verbs are indicated by a (v) after the English, for example:

ernten • harvest (v)

Each language also has its own index at the back of the book. Here you can look up a word in either of the two languages and be referred to the page number(s) where it appears. The gender is shown using the following abbreviations:

m = masculine
f = feminine
n = neuter

die Benutzung des Buchs

how to use this book

Ganz gleich, ob Sie eine Sprache aus Geschäftsgründen, zum Vergnügen oder als Vorbereitung für einen Auslandsurlaub lernen, oder Ihr Vokabular in einer Ihnen bereits vertrauten Sprache erweitern möchten, dieses Wörterbuch ist ein wertvolles Lernmittel, das Sie auf vielfältige Art und Weise benutzen können.

Wenn Sie eine neue Sprache lernen, achten Sie auf Wörter, die in verschiedenen Sprachen ähnlich sind sowie auf falsche Freunde (Wörter, die ähnlich aussehen aber wesentlich andere Bedeutungen haben). Sie können ebenfalls feststellen, wie die Sprachen einander beeinflusst haben. Englisch hat zum Beispiel viele Ausdrücke für Nahrungsmittel aus anderen europäischen Sprachen übernommen und andererseits viele Begriffe aus der Technik und Popkultur ausgeführt.

Praktische Übungen
• Versuchen Sie sich zu Hause, am Arbeits- oder Studienplatz den Inhalt der Seiten einzuprägen, die Ihre Umgebung behandeln. Schließen Sie dann das Buch und prüfen Sie, wie viele Gegenstände Sie in den anderen Sprachen sagen können.
• Schreiben Sie eine Geschichte, einen Brief oder Dialog und benutzen Sie dabei möglichst viele Ausdrücke von einer bestimmten Seite des Wörterbuchs. Dies ist eine gute Methode, sich das Vokabular und die Schreibweise einzuprägen. Sie können mit kurzen Sätzen von zwei bis drei Worten anfangen und dann nach und nach längere Texte schreiben.
• Wenn Sie ein visuelles Gedächtnis haben, können Sie Gegenstände aus dem Buch abzeichnen oder abpausen. Schließen Sie dann das Buch und schreiben Sie die passenden Wörter unter die Bilder.
• Wenn Sie mehr Sicherheit haben, können Sie Wörter aus einem der Fremdsprachenregister aussuchen und deren Bedeutung aufschreiben, bevor Sie auf der entsprechenden Seite nachsehen.

Whether you are learning a new language for business, pleasure, or in preparation for n overseas vacation, or are hoping to extend your vocabulary in an already familiar language, this dictionary is a valuable learning tool that you can use in a number of different ways.

When learning a new language, look for cognates (words that are alike in different languages) and "false friends" (words that look alike but carry significantly different meanings). You can also see where the languages have influenced each other. For example, English has imported many terms for food from other European languages but, in turn, exported terms used in technology and popular culture.

Practical learning activities
• As you move around your home, workplace, or school, try looking at the pages which cover that setting. You could then close the book, look around you, and see how many of the objects and features you can name.
• Challenge yourself to write a story, letter, or dialogue using as many of the terms on a particular page as possible. This will help you retain the vocabulary and remember the spelling. If you want to build up to writing a longer text, start with sentences incorporating 2–3 words.
• If you have a very visual memory, try drawing or tracing items from the book onto a piece of paper, then closing the book and filling in the words below the picture.
• Once you are more confident, pick out words in a foreign-language index and see if you know what they mean before turning to the relevant page to check if you were right.

die Menschen
people

der Körper • body

der Hals
neck

die Brustwarze
nipple

der Kopf
head

die Brust
chest

die Brust
breast

die Taille
waist

der Bauch
abdomen

der Nabel
navel

die Hüfte
hip

der Unterarm
forearm

die Geschlechtsteile
genitals

die Leiste
groin

der Oberschenkel
thigh

das Knie
knee

das Schienbein
shin

das Bein
leg

der Fuß
foot

der Mann
male

die Frau
female

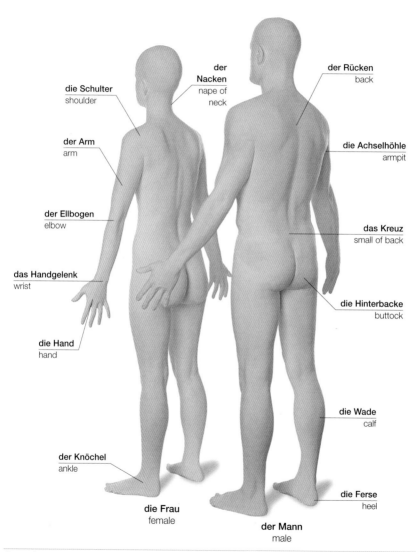

die Schulter
shoulder

der
Nacken
nape of
neck

der Rücken
back

der Arm
arm

die Achselhöhle
armpit

der Ellbogen
elbow

das Kreuz
small of back

das Handgelenk
wrist

die Hinterbacke
buttock

die Hand
hand

die Wade
calf

der Knöchel
ankle

die Frau
female

die Ferse
heel

der Mann
male

das Gesicht • face

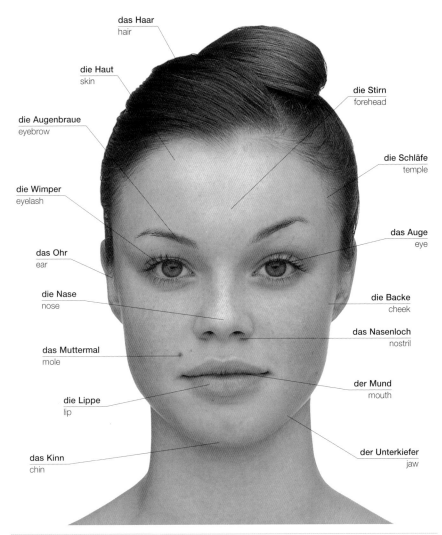

das Haar
hair

die Haut
skin

die Stirn
forehead

die Augenbraue
eyebrow

die Schläfe
temple

die Wimper
eyelash

das Auge
eye

das Ohr
ear

die Nase
nose

die Backe
cheek

das Nasenloch
nostril

das Muttermal
mole

der Mund
mouth

die Lippe
lip

das Kinn
chin

der Unterkiefer
jaw

die Falte
wrinkle

die Sommersprosse
freckle

die Pore
pore

das Grübchen
dimple

die Hand • hand

der
Ringfinger
ring finger

der Mittelfinger
middle finger

der Zeigefinger
index finger

der Fingernagel
nail

die
Nagelhaut
cuticle

der kleine Finger
little finger

der
Daumen
thumb

der
Handknöchel
knuckle

das Handgelenk
wrist

die Handfläche
palm

die Faust
fist

der Fuß • foot

der Ballen
ball

der große Zeh
big toe

der Zehennagel
toenail

der Zeh
toe

die Ferse
heel

der Fußrücken
bridge

der kleine Zeh
little toe

die Fußsohle
sole

das Gewölbe
arch

der Spann
instep

der Knöchel
ankle

die Muskeln • muscles

der Stirnmuskel
frontal

der Deltamuskel
deltoid

der Kapuzenmuskel
trapezius

der Zwischenrip
penmuskel
intercostal

der Brustmuskel
pectoral

der Rückenmuskel
latissimus dorsi

der Bizeps
biceps

der Trizeps
triceps

die
Bauchmuskeln
abdominals

der
Kniesehnen
strang
hamstring

der
Gesäßmuskel
buttock

die
Oberschenkel
muskeln
quadriceps

die
Achillessehne
Achilles tendon

der
Wadenmuskel
calf

das Skelett • skeleton

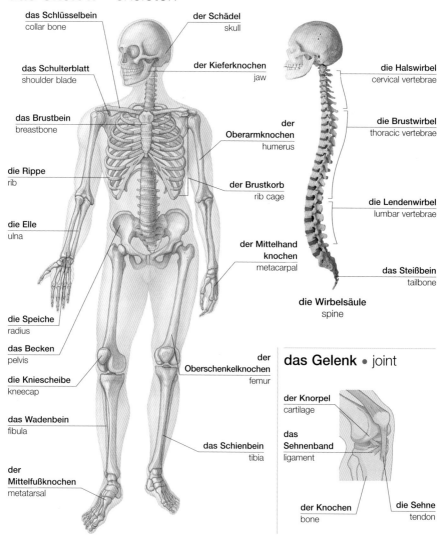

das Schlüsselbein
collar bone

der Schädel
skull

das Schulterblatt
shoulder blade

der Kieferknochen
jaw

die Halswirbel
cervical vertebrae

das Brustbein
breastbone

der
Oberarmknochen
humerus

die Brustwirbel
thoracic vertebrae

die Rippe
rib

der Brustkorb
rib cage

die Elle
ulna

die Lendenwirbel
lumbar vertebrae

der Mittelhand
knochen
metacarpal

das Steißbein
tailbone

die Speiche
radius

die Wirbelsäule
spine

das Becken
pelvis

der
Oberschenkelknochen
femur

das Gelenk • joint

die Kniescheibe
kneecap

der Knorpel
cartilage

das Wadenbein
fibula

das
Sehnenband
ligament

das Schienbein
tibia

der
Mittelfußknochen
metatarsal

der Knochen
bone

die Sehne
tendon

die inneren Organe • internal organs

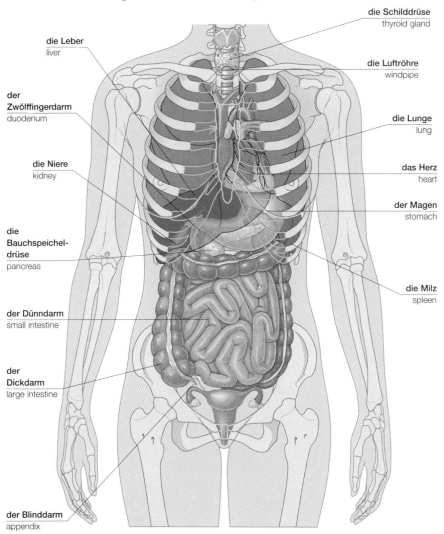

die Schilddrüse
thyroid gland

die Leber
liver

die Luftröhre
windpipe

der
Zwölffingerdarm
duodenum

die Lunge
lung

die Niere
kidney

das Herz
heart

der Magen
stomach

die
Bauchspeichel-
drüse
pancreas

der Dünndarm
small intestine

die Milz
spleen

der
Dickdarm
large intestine

der Blinddarm
appendix

der Kopf • head

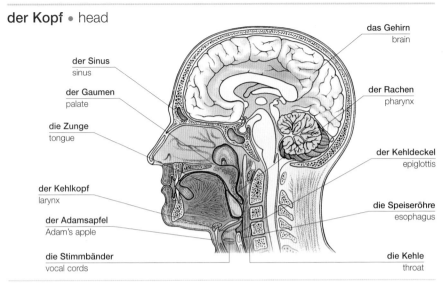

das Gehirn
brain

der Sinus
sinus

der Gaumen
palate

die Zunge
tongue

der Rachen
pharynx

der Kehlkopf
larynx

der Adamsapfel
Adam's apple

die Stimmbänder
vocal cords

der Kehldeckel
epiglottis

die Speiseröhre
esophagus

die Kehle
throat

die Körpersysteme • body systems

das Zwerchfell
diaphragm

die Vene
vein

die Arterie
artery

das Atmungssystem
respiratory

das Verdauungssystem
digestive

das Herz- und
Gefäßsystem
cardiovascular

das lymphatische
System
lymphatic

die Drüse
gland

der Nerv
nerve

das Harnsystem
urinary

das endokrine System
endocrine

das Nervensystem
nervous

das Fortpflanzungssystem
reproductive

die Fortpflanzungsorgane • reproductive organs

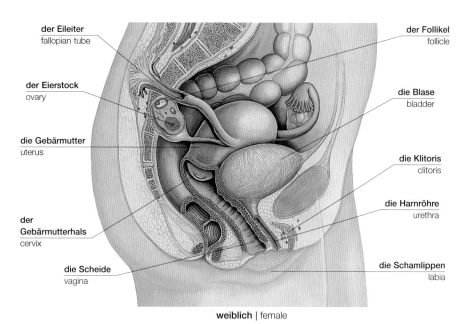

der Eileiter
fallopian tube

der Follikel
follicle

der Eierstock
ovary

die Blase
bladder

die Gebärmutter
uterus

die Klitoris
clitoris

die Harnröhre
urethra

der
Gebärmutterhals
cervix

die Scheide
vagina

die Schamlippen
labia

weiblich | female

die Fortpflanzung • reproduction

das Spermium
sperm

das Ei
egg

die Befruchtung | fertilization

Vokabular • vocabulary

steril infertile	**impotent** impotent	**die Menstruation** menstruation
fruchtbar fertile	**empfangen** conceive	**der Geschlechtsverkehr** intercourse
das Hormon hormone	**der Eisprung** ovulation	**die Geschlechtskrankheit** sexually transmitted disease

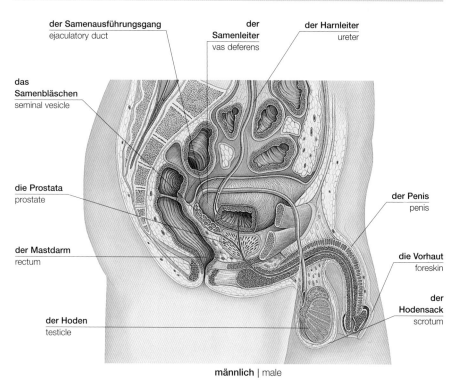

der Samenausführungsgang
ejaculatory duct

der Samenleiter
vas deferens

der Harnleiter
ureter

das Samenbläschen
seminal vesicle

die Prostata
prostate

der Penis
penis

der Mastdarm
rectum

die Vorhaut
foreskin

der Hodensack
scrotum

der Hoden
testicle

männlich | male

die Empfängnisverhütung • contraception

das Pessar
cervical cap

das Diaphragma
diaphragm

das Kondom
condom

die Spirale
IUD

die Pille
pill

die Familie • family

die Großmutter
grandmother

der Großvater
grandfather

der Onkel
uncle

die Tante
aunt

der Vater
father

die Mutter
mother

der Cousin
cousin

der Bruder
brother

die Schwester
sister

die Ehefrau
wife

die Schwiegertochter
daughter-in-law

der Sohn
son

die Tochter
daughter

der Schwiegersohn
son-in-law

der Enkel
grandson

die Enkelin
granddaughter

der Ehemann
husband

Vokabular • vocabulary

die Großeltern grandparents	die Verwandten relatives	die Enkelkinder grandchildren	die Stiefmutter stepmother	die Stieftochter stepdaughter	die Generation generation
die Eltern parents	die Kinder children	der Stiefvater stepfather	der Stiefsohn stepson	der Partner/die Partnerin partner	die Zwillinge twins

die
Schwiegermutter
mother-in-law

der
Schwiegervater
father-in-law

der Schwager
brother-in-law

die Schwägerin
sister-in-law

die Nichte
niece

der Neffe
nephew

die Anreden • titles

Frau
Mrs.

Herr
Mr.

Fräulein
Miss

die Stadien • stages

das Baby
baby

das Kind
child

der Junge
boy

das Mädchen
girl

die Jugendliche
teenager

der Erwachsene
adult

der Mann
man

die Frau
woman

die Beziehungen • relationships

der Chef | manager
die Assistentin | assistant
die Geschäftspartnerin | business partner
die Arbeitgeberin | employer
der Arbeitnehmer | employee
der Kollege | colleague

das Büro | office

der Nachbar | neighbor

der Freund | friend

der Bekannte | acquaintance

der Brieffreund | pen pal

der Freund | boyfriend
die Freundin | girlfriend
der Verlobte | fiancé
die Verlobte | fiancée

das Paar | couple

die Verlobten | engaged couple

die Gefühle • emotions

das Lächeln
smile

glücklich
happy

traurig
sad

aufgeregt
excited

gelangweilt
bored

überrascht
surprised

erschrocken
scared

das Stirnrunzeln
frown

verärgert
angry

verwirrt
confused

besorgt
worried

nervös
nervous

stolz
proud

selbstsicher
confident

verlegen
embarrassed

schüchtern
shy

Vokabular • vocabulary

bestürzt upset	**schreien** shout (v)	**lachen** laugh (v)	**seufzen** sigh (v)
schockiert shocked	**gähnen** yawn (v)	**weinen** cry (v)	**in Ohnmacht fallen** faint (v)

die Ereignisse des Lebens • life events

geboren werden
be born (v)

zur Schule kommen
start school (v)

sich befreunden
make friends (v)

graduieren
graduate (v)

eine Stelle bekommen
get a job (v)

sich verlieben
fall in love (v)

heiraten
get married (v)

ein Baby bekommen
have a baby (v)

die Hochzeit | wedding

die Scheidung
divorce

das Begräbnis
funeral

vokabular • vocabulary

die Taufe christening	**emigrieren** emigrate (v)
die Bar Mizwa bar mitzvah	**sterben** die (v)
der Hochzeitstag anniversary	**die Hochzeitsfeier** wedding reception
in den Ruhestand treten retire (v)	**die Hochzeitsreise** honeymoon
sein Testament machen make a will (v)	**die Geburtsurkunde** birth certificate

die Feste • celebrations

die
Geburtstagsfeier
birthday party

die Karte
card

die Feste •
festivals

der Geburtstag
birthday

das Geschenk
present

das Weihnachten
Christmas

das Passah
Passover

das Neujahr
New Year

der Karneval
carnival

der Umzug
procession

der Ramadan
Ramadan

das Band
ribbon

der Thanksgiving Day
Thanksgiving

das Ostern
Easter

das Halloween
Halloween

das Diwali
Diwali

die äußere Erscheinung
appearance

die Kinderkleidung • children's clothing

das Baby • baby

der Schneeanzug
snowsuit

das
Hemdchen
undershirt

der
Druckknopf
snap

der
Strampelanzug
coverall

der Schlafanzug
sleeper

der Spielanzug
romper

das Lätzchen
bib

die
Babyhandschuhe
mittens

die
Babyschuhe
booties

die
Stoffwindel
cloth diaper

die
Wegwerfwindel
disposable diaper

das
Gummihöschen
plastic pants

das Kleinkind • toddler

das T-Shirt
T-shirt

die Latzhose
overalls

der Sonnenhut
sun hat

die Schürze
apron

die Shorts
shorts

der Rock
skirt

das Kind • child

das Kleid
dress

die Kapuze
hood

die Jeans
jeans

der Rucksack
backpack

der Kne-
belknopf
toggle

der Schal
scarf

der
Anorak
parka

die
Sandalen
sandals

die
Gummistiefel
wellington
boots

der Sommer
summer

der Regenmantel
raincoat

der Herbst
fall

der Dufflecoat
duffle coat

der Winter
winter

der Morgenrock
bathrobe

das Logo
logo

die
Sportschuhe
athletic shoes

das Nachthemd
nightgown

die Hausschuhe
slippers

die Nachtwäsche
nightwear

der Fußballdress
soccer uniform

der Trainingsanzug
jogging suit

die Leggings
leggings

Vokabular • vocabulary

die Naturfaser
natural fiber

synthetisch
synthetic

Ist es waschmaschinenfest?
Is it machine washable?

Passt das einem
Zweijährigen?
Will this fit a two-year-old?

die Herrenkleidung • men's clothing

der Kragen
collar

die Krawatte
tie

der Gürtel
belt

das Revers
lapel

das Knopfloch
buttonhole

die Manschette
cuff

die Jacke
jacket

die Hose
pants

der Knopf
button

die Tasche
pocket

der Straßenanzug
business suit

der Regenmantel
raincoat

das Futter
lining

die Leder schuhe
leather shoes

Vokabular • vocabulary

das Hemd shirt	**der Bademantel** bathrobe	**der Mantel** coat	**lang** long
die Strickjacke cardigan	**die Unterwäsche** underwear	**der Trainingsanzug** jogging suit	**kurz** short

Haben Sie das eine Nummer größer/kleiner?
Do you have this in a larger/smaller size?

Kann ich das anprobieren?
May I try this on?

der Blazer
blazer

das Sportjackett
sport coat

die Weste
waistcoat

der V-Ausschnitt
V-neck

der runde
Ausschnitt
round neck

das T-Shirt
T-shirt

der Anorak
parka

das Sweatshirt
sweatshirt

die Windjacke
windbreaker

die Trainings
hose
sweatpants

der Pullover
sweater

der Schlafanzug
pajamas

das Unterhemd
vest

die Freizeitkleidung
casual wear

die Shorts
shorts

der Slip
briefs

die Boxershorts
boxer shorts

die Socken
socks

die Damenkleidung • women's clothing

der Ausschnitt
neckline

trägerlos
strapless

die Jacke
jacket

die Naht
seam

ärmellos
sleeveless

der Ärmel
sleeve

knöchellang
ankle length

das Abendkleid
evening dress

das Kleid
dress

der Rock
skirt

die Bluse
blouse

knielang
knee-length

die Hose
pants

der Saum
hem

die Strumpfhose
pantyhose

die Schuhe
shoes

leger
casual

die Unterwäsche • lingerie

das Negligé
negligée

der Unterrock
slip

der Träger
strap

das Mieder
camisole

das Bustier
bustier

der
Strumpfhalter
suspender belt

die Strümpfe
stockings

die Strumpfhose
pantyhose

das
Unterhemd
vest

der Büstenhalter
bra

der Slip
panties

das Nachthemd
nightgown

die Hochzeit • wedding

der Schleier
veil

die
Spitze
lace

das Bukett
bouquet

die
Schleppe
train

das Hochzeitskleid
wedding dress

Vokabular • vocabulary

das Korsett corset	**gut geschnitten** tailored
rückenfrei halter neck	**das Strumpfband** garter
der Rockbund waistband	**der Sport-BH** sports bra
das Schulter polster shoulder pad	**mit Formbügeln** underwired

die Accessoires • accessories

die
Gürtelschnalle
buckle

der Griff
handle

die Mütze
cap

der Hut
hat

das Halstuch
scarf

der Gürtel
belt

die Spitze
tip

das Taschentuch
handkerchief

die Fliege
bow tie

die
Krawattennadel
tie-pin

die Handschuhe
gloves

der Regenschirm
umbrella

der Schmuck • jewelry

die Perlenkette
string of pearls

der Anhänger
pendant

die Brosche
brooch

der Manschettenknopf
cufflink

das Glied
link

der Verschluß
clasp

der Ohrring
earring

der Ring
ring

der Edelstein
stone

die Halskette
necklace

die Uhr
watch

das Armband
bracelet

die Kette
chain

der Schmuckkasten | jewelry box

die Taschen • bags

der Verschluss
fastening

der
Schulterriemen
shoulder strap

die Griffe
handles

die Brieftasche
wallet

**das
Portemonnaie**
purse

**die
Umhängetasche**
shoulder bag

die Reisetasche
duffle bag

die Aktentasche
briefcase

die Handtasche
handbag

der Rucksack
backpack

die Schuhe • shoes

der Schnürsenkel
lace

die Zunge
tongue

die Öse
eyelet

die Sohle
sole

der Absatz
heel

der Schnürschuh
lace-up

der Wanderschuh
walking boot

der Sportschuh
athletic shoe

der Lederschuh
leather shoe

die Strandsandale
flip-flop

**der Schuh mit
hohem Absatz**
high-heeled shoe

der Plateauschuh
platform shoe

die Sandale
sandal

der Slipper
slip-on

**der
Herrenhalbschuh**
oxford

das Haar • hair

der Kamm
comb

kämmen
comb (v)

die Haarbürste
brush

bürsten | brush (v)

die Friseurin
hairdresser

das Waschbecken
sink

die Kundin
client

waschen | wash (v)

der Frisierumhang
robe

ausspülen
rinse (v)

schneiden
cut (v)

föhnen
blow-dry (v)

legen
set (v)

---

die Frisierartikel • accessories

der Föhn
hairdryer

das Shampoo
shampoo

die Haarspülung
conditioner

das Haargel
gel

das Haarspray
hairspray

der Lockenstab
curling iron

die Schere
scissors

der Haarreif
headband

der Lockenwickler
curler

die Haarklammer
hairpin

die Frisuren • styles

das
Band
ribbon

der Pferdeschwanz
ponytail

der Zopf
braid

die Hochfrisur
French braid

der Haarknoten
bun

die Schwänzchen
pigtails

der Bubikopf
bob

der Kurzhaarschnitt
crop

kraus
curly

die Dauerwelle
perm

glatt
straight

die **Wurzeln**
roots

die Strähnen
highlights

kahl
bald

die Perücke
wig

Vokabular • vocabulary	
das Haarband hairband	**fettig** greasy
nachschneiden trim (v)	**trocken** dry
der Herrenfriseur barber	**normal** normal
die Schuppen dandruff	**die Kopfhaut** scalp
der Haarspliss split ends	**glätten** straighten (v)

die Haarfarben • colors

blond
blonde

brünett
brunette

rotbraun
auburn

rot
red

schwarz
black

grau
grey

weiß
white

gefärbt
dyed

die Schönheit • beauty

das Haarfärbemittel
hair dye

der Lidschatten
eyeshadow

die Wimperntusche
mascara

der Eyeliner
eyeliner

das Puderrouge
blusher

die Grundierung
foundation

der Lippenstift
lipstick

das Make-up • makeup

der Augenbrauenstift
eyebrow pencil

das Brauenbürstchen
eyebrow brush

die Pinzette
tweezers

das Lipgloss
lip gloss

der Lippenpinsel
lip brush

der Lippenkonturenstift
lip liner

der Puderpinsel
brush

der Korrekturstift
concealer

der Spiegel
mirror

der Gesichtspuder
face powder

die Puderquaste
powder puff

die Puderdose | compact

die Schönheitsbehandlungen •
beauty treatments

die Toilettenartikel • toiletries

die
Gesichtsmaske
face mask

die Sonnenbank
sunbed

die Haut schälen
exfoliate (v)

die
Gesichtsbehandlung
facial

die Enthaarung
wax

die Pediküre
pedicure

der Reiniger
cleanser

**das Gesichts-
wasser**
toner

**die Feuchtig-
keitscreme**
moisturizer

**die Selbst-
bräunungscreme**
self-tanning cream

**das
Parfum**
perfume

**das Eau de
Toilette**
cologne

die Maniküre • manicure

der Nagellackentferner
nail polish remover

die Nagelfeile
nail file

der Nagellack
nail polish

die
Nagelschere
nail scissors

der
Nagelknipser
nail clippers

Vokabular • vocabulary

die Sonnenbräune tan	**empfindlich** sensitive	**hell** fair
die Tätowierung tattoo	**der Farbton** shade	**dunkel** dark
die Wattebällchen cotton balls	**Antifalten-** antiwrinkle	**trocken** dry
hypoallergen hypoallergenic	**der Teint** complexion	**fettig** oily

die Gesundheit
health

die Krankheit • illness

die Kopfschmerzen
headache

das Nasenbluten
nosebleed

der Husten
cough

das Fieber | fever

das Niesen
sneeze

die Erkältung
cold

die Grippe
flu

der Inhalations apparat
inhaler

das Asthma
asthma

die Krämpfe
cramps

die Übelkeit
nausea

die Windpocken
chickenpox

der Hautausschlag
rash

Vokabular • vocabulary

der Herzinfarkt heart attack	die Allergie allergy	das Ekzem eczema	die Verkühlung chill	die Epilepsie epilepsy	der Durchfall diarrhea
der Blutdruck blood pressure	der Mumps mumps	der Virus virus	die Migräne migraine	sich übergeben vomit (v)	die Masern measles
der Schlaganfall stroke	die Zucker krankheit diabetes	die Infektion infection	die Magenschmerzen stomachache	in Ohnmacht fallen faint (v)	der Heuschnupfen hayfever

der Arzt • doctor
die Konsultation • consultation

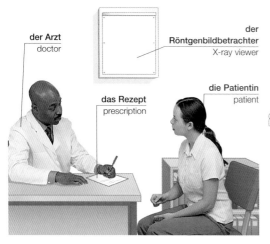

der Arzt
doctor

**der
Röntgenbildbetrachter**
X-ray viewer

das Rezept
prescription

die Patientin
patient

der Körpergrößenmesser
height bar

**die Kranken
schwester**
nurse

**die
Personenwaage**
scale

der Blutdruckmesser
blood pressure gauge

das Stethoskop
stethoscope

die Luftmanschette
cuff

Vokabular • vocabulary

der Termin
appointment

die Impfung
vaccination

**das
Sprechzimmer**
surgery

die Untersuchung
medical
examination

der Warteraum
waiting room

das Thermometer
thermometer

**Ich muss mit einem Arzt
sprechen.**
I need to see a doctor.

Es tut hier weh.
It hurts here.

die Verletzung • injury

die Schlinge
sling

die Halskrawatte
neck brace

die Fraktur
fracture

das Schleudertrauma
whiplash

die Verstauchung | sprain

der Schnitt
cut

die Abschürfung
graze

die Prellung
bruise

der Splitter
splinter

der Sonnenbrand
sunburn

die Brandwunde
burn

der Biss
bite

der Stich
sting

Vokabular • vocabulary

der Unfall accident	**die Blutung** hemorrhage	**die Kopfverletzung** head injury	**Wird er/sie es gut überstehen?** Will he/she be all right?
der Notfall emergency	**die Blase** blister	**die Vergiftung** poisoning	**Rufen Sie bitte einen Krankenwagen.** Please call an ambulance.
die Wunde wound	**der elektrische Schlag** electric shock	**die Gehirnerschütterung** concussion	**Wo haben Sie Schmerzen?** Where does it hurt?

---

die erste Hilfe • first aid

die Salbe
ointment

das
Desinfektionstuch
antiseptic wipe

das Pflaster
adhesive
bandage

die
Sicherheitsnadel
safety pin

die Pinzette
tweezers

die Bandage
bandage

die Schere
scissors

die Schmerz
tabletten
painkillers

das Antiseptikum
antiseptic

der Erste-Hilfe-Kasten | first aid box

die Gaze
gauze

der Verband
dressing

die Schiene | splint

das Leukoplast
adhesive tape

die Wiederbelebung
resuscitation

Vokabular • vocabulary			
der Schock shock	**der Puls** pulse	**ersticken** choke (v)	**Können Sie mir helfen?** Can you help?
bewusstlos unconscious	**die Atmung** breathing	**steril** sterile	**Beherrschen Sie die Erste Hilfe?** Do you know first aid?

das Krankenhaus • hospital

der Chirurg
surgeon

die Kranken-
schwester
nurse

der Operationssaal
operating room

die
Patiententabelle
chart

der Anästhesist
anesthetist

die Blutuntersuchung
blood test

die Spritze
injection

die Röntgenaufnahme
X-ray

die
fahrbare Liege
gurney

die Notaufnahme
emergency room

der Rufknopf
call button

die
Krankenhausstation
ward

der Rollstuhl
wheelchair

der CT-Scan
scan

Vokabular • vocabulary

die Operation	entlassen	die Besuchszeiten	die Entbindungsstation	die Intensivstation
operation	discharged	visiting hours	maternity ward	intensive care unit
aufgenommen	die Klinik	die Kinderstation	das Privatzimmer	der ambulante Patient
admitted	clinic	children's ward	private room	outpatient

die Abteilungen • departments

die HNO-Abteilung
ENT (otolaryngology)

die Kardiologie
cardiology

die Orthopädie
orthopedics

die Gynäkologie
gynecology

die Physiotherapie
physiotherapy

die Dermatologie
dermatology

die Pädiatrie
pediatrics

die Radiologie
radiology

die Chirurgie
surgery

die Entbindungsstation
maternity

die Psychiatrie
psychiatry

die Ophthalmologie
ophthalmology

Vokabular • vocabulary

die Neurologie neurology	**die Urologie** urology	**die plastische Chirurgie** plastic surgery	**die Pathologie** pathology	**das Ergebnis** result
die Onkologie oncology	**die Endokrinologie** endocrinology	**die Überweisung** referral	**die Untersuchung** test	**der Facharzt** specialist

---

der Zahnarzt • dentist

der Zahn • tooth

der Zahn
schmelz
enamel

das
Zahnfleisch
gum

der Nerv
nerve

die
Zahnwurzel
root

der vordere
Backenzahn
premolar

der
Schneidezahn
incisor

der
Backen-
zahn
molar

der Eckzahn
canine

Vokabular • vocabulary

der Zahnbelag
plaque

der Bohrer
drill

die Karies
decay

die Zahnseide
dental floss

die Zahnfüllung
filling

die Extraktion
extraction

die
Zahnschmerzen
toothache

die Krone
crown

der Check-up • checkup

die Behandlungslampe
reflector

die Sonde
probe

die Behandlungsschürze
apron

das Speibecken
sink

der Patientenstuhl
dentist's chair

mit Zahnseide
reinigen
floss (v)

bürsten
brush

die Zahnspange
brace

die Röntgen-
aufnahme
dental X-ray

das Röntgenbild
X-ray film

die
Zahnprothese
dentures

---

der Augenoptiker • optometrist

das Futteral
case

das Glas
lens

das Brillengestell
frame

die Brille
glasses

die Sonnenbrille
sunglasses

das Reinigungsmittel
cleaning fluid

das
Desinfektionsmittel
disinfectant solution

der
Kontaktlinsen
behälter
lens case

der Sehtest | eye test

die Kontaktlinsen | contact lenses

das Auge • eye

die Augenbraue
eyebrow

das Lid
eyelid

die Wimper
eyelash

die Pupille
pupil

die Iris
iris

die Netzhaut
retina

die Linse
lens

der Sehnerv
optic nerve

die Hornhaut
cornea

Vokabular • vocabulary	
die Sehkraft vision	**der Astigmatismus** astigmatism
die Dioptrie diopter	**die Weitsichtigkeit** farsightedness
die Träne tear	**die Kurzsichtigkeit** nearsightedness
der graue Star cataract	**Bifokal-** bifocal

die Schwangerschaft • pregnancy

die Kranken-
schwester
nurse

der Schwangerschaftstest
pregnancy test

die
Ultraschallaufnahme
scan

die Plazenta
placenta

die
Nabelschnur
umbilical cord

der
Gebärmutterhals
cervix

die
Gebärmutter
uterus

der Ultraschall | ultrasound

der Fetus | fetus

Vokabular • vocabulary

der Eisprung ovulation	vorgeburtlich prenatal	das Fruchtwasser amniotic fluid	die Erweiterung dilation	die Naht stitches	Steiß- breech
schwanger pregnant	der Embryo embryo	die Amniozentese amniocentesis	der Kaiserschnitt cesarean section	die Geburt birth	vorzeitig premature
die Empfängnis conception	die Gebärmutter womb	das Fruchtwasser geht ab break water (v)	die Periduralanästhesie epidural	die Entbindung delivery	der Gynäkologe gynecologist
schwanger expecting	das Trimester trimester	die Wehe contraction	der Dammschnitt episiotomy	die Fehlgeburt miscarriage	der Geburtshelfer obstetrician

---

die Geburt • childbirth

die Tropfinfusion
drip

die Hebamme
midwife

der Monitor
monitor

der Katheter
catheter

die Geburt einleiten
induce labor (v)

der Brutkasten | incubator

die Waage
scale

das Geburtsgewicht | birth weight

die Geburtszange
forceps

die Saugglocke
suction cup

die assistierte Entbindung
assisted delivery

das Erkennungsetikett
identity tag

das Neugeborene
newborn baby

das Stillen • nursing

die Brustpumpe
breast pump

der Stillbüstenhalter
nursing bra

stillen
breastfeed (v)

die Einlagen
pads

die Alternativtherapien • complementary therapy

der Lehrer
teacher

die Massage
massage

das Shiatsu
shiatsu

das Yoga | yoga

die Matte
mat

die Chiropraktik
chiropractic

die Osteopathie
osteopathy

die Reflexzonenmassage
reflexology

die Meditation
meditation

der Berater
counselor

die Gruppentherapie
group therapy

das Reiki
reiki

die Akupunktur
acupuncture

das Ayurveda
ayurveda

die Hypnotherapie
hypnotherapy

die ätherischen Öle
essential oils

die Kräuterheilkunde
herbalism

die Aromatherapie
aromatherapy

die Homöopathie
homeopathy

die Akupressur
acupressure

die Therapeutin
therapist

die Psychotherapie
psychotherapy

Vokabular • vocabulary

die Kristalltherapie crystal healing	**die Naturheilkunde** naturopathy	**die Entspannung** relaxation	**das Heilkraut** herb
die Wasserbehandlung hydrotherapy	**das Feng Shui** feng shui	**der Stress** stress	**die Ergänzung** supplement

---

das Haus
home

das Haus • house

das Dach
roof

die Dachrinne
gutter

der Schornstein
chimney

das Mansardenfenster
dormer window

die Mauer
wall

der Dachvorsprung
eaves

der Dachziegel
shingle

der Fensterladen
shutter

das Vordach
porch

das Fenster
window

der Anbau
extension

der Weg
sidewalk

die Haustür
front door

Vokabular • vocabulary

Einzel(haus) single-family	**Reihen(haus)** row house	**die Garage** garage	**das Stockwerk** floor	**die Alarmanlage** burglar alarm	**mieten** rent (v)
Doppel(haus) duplex	**der Bungalow** ranch house	**das Zimmer** room	**der Hof** courtyard	**der Briefkasten** mailbox	**die Miete** rent
das dreistöckige Haus townhouse	**das Kellergeschoss** basement	**der Dachboden** attic	**die Haustürlampe** porch light	**der Vermieter** landlord	**der Mieter** tenant

der Eingang • entrance

die Wohnung •
apartment

das Geländer
hand rail

der Treppen-absatz
landing

das Treppen-geländer
banister

die Treppe
staircase

die Diele
foyer

der Balkon
balcony

der Wohnblock
apartment building

die Sprechanlage
intercom

die Türklingel
doorbell

der Fußabtreter
doormat

der Türklopfer
door knocker

der Schlüssel
key

der Fahrstuhl
elevator

die Türkette
door chain

das Schloss
lock

der Türriegel
bolt

die Hausanschlüsse • internal systems

der Flügel
blade

der Ventilator
fan

der Heizlüfter
convector heater

der Heizkörper
radiator

der Heizofen
space heater

---

die Elektrizität • electricity

der Glühfaden
filament

die Erdung
ground

der Pol
pin

neutral
neutral

die Bajonettfassung
base

geladen
live

die Birne
light bulb

der Stecker
plug

die Leitung
wires

Vokabular • vocabulary

die Spannung voltage	**die Sicherung** fuse	**die Steckdose** outlet	**der Gleichstrom** direct current	**der Transformator** transformer
das Ampère amp	**der Generator** generator	**der Schalter** switch	**der Stromzähler** electric meter	**das Stromnetz** household current
der Strom power	**der Sicherungskasten** fuse box	**der Wechselstrom** alternating current	**der Stromausfall** power outage	

---

deutsch • english

die Installation • plumbing

die Zuleitung
inlet

der Auslass
outlet

das Sicherheits ventil
pressure valve

die Isolierung
insulation

der Überlauf
overflow pipe

der Kessel
tank

der Wasser raum
water chamber

der Ablass hahn
drain cock

der Thermostat
thermostat

der Gasbrenner
gas burner

das Heizelement
heating element

der Boiler
water heater

die Spüle • sink

der Hahn
faucet

der Hebel
lever

die Dichtung
gasket

die Zuleitung
supply pipe

der Absperrhahn
shutoff valve

der Abfluss
drain

der Müllschlucker
waste disposal unit

das WC • toilet

der Spülkasten
tank

der Schwimmer
float ball

der Toiletten sitz
seat

das Abflussrohr
waste pipe

das Becken
bowl

die Abfallentsorgung • waste disposal

die Flasche
bottle

der Deckel
lid

der Trethebel
pedal

der Recyclingbehälter
recycling bin

der Abfalleimer
garbage can

die Abfallsortiereinheit
sorting unit

der Bio-Abfall
organic waste

das Wohnzimmer • living room

das Gemälde
painting

der
Bilderrahmen
frame

die Lampe
lamp

die
Wandlampe
wall light

die Uhr
clock

die Decke
ceiling

die Vitrine
cabinet

das Sofa
sofa

das
Sofakissen
cushion

der
Couchtisch
coffee table

der Fußboden
floor

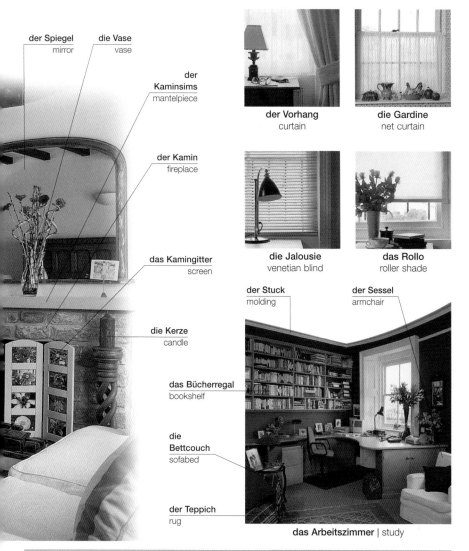

der Spiegel
mirror

die Vase
vase

der
Kaminsims
mantelpiece

der Kamin
fireplace

das Kamingitter
screen

die Kerze
candle

das Bücherregal
bookshelf

die
Bettcouch
sofabed

der Teppich
rug

der Vorhang
curtain

die Gardine
net curtain

die Jalousie
venetian blind

das Rollo
roller shade

der Stuck
molding

der Sessel
armchair

das Arbeitszimmer | study

das Esszimmer • dining room

der Pfeffer
pepper

das Salz
salt

der Tisch
table

das Geschirr
crockery

das Besteck
cutlery

der Stuhl
chair

die Lehne
back

die Sitzfläche
seat

das Bein
leg

Vokabular • vocabulary

die Tischdecke tablecloth	**die Gastgeberin** hostess	**die Portion** portion	**den Tisch decken** set the table (v)	**das Frühstück** breakfast	**Könnte ich bitte noch ein bisschen haben?** Can I have some more, please?
das Set placemat	**der Gast** guest	**hungrig** hungry	**servieren** serve (v)	**das Mittagessen** lunch	**Ich bin satt, danke.** I've had enough, thank you.
das Essen meal	**der Gastgeber** host	**satt** full	**essen** eat (v)	**das Abendessen** dinner	**Das war lecker.** That was delicious.

das Geschirr und das Besteck • crockery and cutlery

der Becher
mug

die Kaffeetasse
coffee cup

der Teelöffel
teaspoon

die Teetasse
teacup

der Teller
plate

die Schüssel
bowl

die Cafetière
cafetière

die Teekanne
teapot

das Kännchen
jug

der Eierbecher
egg cup

das Weinglas
wine glass

das Wasserglas
tumbler

die Glaswaren
glassware

der Serviettenring
napkin ring

der Beilagenteller
side plate

der Essteller
dinner plate

der Suppenteller
soup bowl

der Suppenlöffel
soup spoon

die Serviette
napkin

die Gabel
fork

das Gedeck
place setting

der Löffel
spoon

das Messer
knife

die Küche • kitchen

das Küchenregal
shelves

der Spritzschutz
backsplash

der Wasserhahn
faucet

das
Spülbecken
sink

die Schublade
drawer

der Dunstabzug
extractor

das
Glaskeramik
kochfeld
ceramic
range

die
Arbeitsfläche
countertop

der Backofen
oven

der Küchen
schrank
cabinet

die Küchengeräte • appliances

die
Mixerschüssel
mixing bowl

der Deckel
lid

die Mikrowelle
microwave oven

das
Messer
blade

der
Elektrokessel
electric kettle

der Toaster
toaster

die
Küchenmaschine
food processor

der Mixer
blender

die Spülmaschine
dishwasher

das
Eisfach
icemaker

der Rost
shelf

das
Gefrierfach
freezer

das
Gemüsefach
crisper

der Gefrier-Kühlschrank | refrigerator

Vokabular • vocabulary

das Kochfeld range	**einfrieren** freeze (v)
das Abtropfbrett draining board	**auftauen** defrost (v)
der Brenner burner	**dämpfen** steam (v)
der Mülleimer garbage can	**anbraten** sauté (v)

das Kochen • cooking

schälen
peel (v)

schneiden
slice (v)

reiben
grate (v)

gießen
pour (v)

verrühren
mix (v)

schlagen
whisk (v)

kochen
boil (v)

braten
fry (v)

ausrollen
roll (v)

rühren
stir (v)

köcheln lassen
simmer (v)

pochieren
poach (v)

backen
bake (v)

braten
roast (v)

grillen
broil (v)

die Küchengeräte • kitchenware

das Hackbrett
cutting board

das Brotmesser
bread knife

das Küchenmesser
kitchen knife

das Hackmesser
cleaver

der Messer-schärfer
knife sharpener

der Fleischklopfer
meat tenderizer

der Spieß
skewer

der Stößel
pestle

der Schäler
vegetable peeler

der Apfelstecher
apple corer

die Reibe
grater

der Mörser
mortar

der Kartoffel-stampfer
masher

der Dosenöffner
can opener

der Flaschenöffner
bottle opener

die Knoblauchpresse
garlic press

der Servierlöffel
serving spoon

der Pfannenwender
slotted spatula

das Sieb
colander

der Spachtel
spatula

der Holzlöffel
wooden spoon

der Schaumlöffel
slotted spoon

der Schöpflöffel
ladle

die Tranchiergabel
carving fork

der Portionierer
ice-cream scoop

der Schneebesen
whisk

das Sieb
sieve

der Deckel
lid

kunststoffbeschichtet
nonstick

die Bratpfanne
frying pan

der Kochtopf
saucepan

das Grillblech
grill pan

der Wok
wok

der Schmortopf
earthenware dish

Glas-
glass

feuerfest
ovenproof

die Rührschüssel
mixing bowl

die Soufflėform
soufflé dish

die Auflaufform
gratin dish

das Auflaufförmchen
ramekin

die Kasserolle
casserole dish

das Kuchenbacken • baking cakes

die Haushaltswaage
scale

der Messbecher
measuring cup

die Kuchenform
cake pan

die Pastetenform
pie pan

die Obstkuchen-form
quiche pan

der Backpinsel
pastry brush

das Nudelholz
rolling pin

der Spritzbeutel
piping bag

die Törtchen-form
muffin pan

das Kuchenblech
baking sheet

das Abkühlgitter
cooling rack

der Topfhandschuh
oven mitt

die Schürze
apron

das Schlafzimmer • bedroom

der Kleiderschrank
wardrobe

die
Nachttisch
lampe
bedside lamp

das Kopfende
headboard

der Nachttisch
nightstand

die Kommode
chest of drawers

die Schublade
drawer

das Bett
bed

die Matratze
mattress

die Tagesdecke
bedspread

das
Kopfkissen
pillow

die
Wärmflasche
hot-water bottle

der
Radiowecker
clock radio

der Wecker
alarm clock

die
Papiertaschen
tuchschachtel
box of tissues

der Kleiderbügel
coat hanger

die Bettwäsche • bed linen

der Spiegel
mirror

der
Frisiertisch
dressing
table

der Kissenbezug
pillowcase

das Bettlaken
sheet

der Volant
dust ruffle

die Bettdecke
comfortert

die Steppdecke
quilt

der
Fußboden
floor

die Decke
blanket

Vokabular • vocabulary

das Einzelbett twin bed	das Fußende footboard	die Schlaflosigkeit insomnia	aufwachen wake up (v)	den Wecker stellen set the alarm (v)
das Doppelbett full bed	die Sprungfeder spring	ins Bett gehen go to bed (v)	aufstehen get up (v)	schnarchen snore (v)
die Heizdecke electric blanket	der Teppich carpet	einschlafen go to sleep (v)	das Bett machen make the bed (v)	der Einbauschrank built-in wardrobe

das Badezimmer • bathroom

der
Handtuchhalter
towel bar

die Duschtür
shower door

der
Kaltwasserhahn
cold faucet

der
Heißwasserhahn
hot faucet

das
Waschbecken
sink

der Duschkopf
shower head

der **Stöpsel**
plug

die Dusche
shower

der Abfluss
drain

der Toilettensitz
toilet seat

die Badewanne
bathtub

die Toilette
toilet

die
Toilettenbürste
toilet brush

das Bidet | bidet

Vokabular • vocabulary

die Hausapotheke
medicine cabinet

die Badematte
bath mat

die Rolle Toilettenpapier
toilet paper

der Duschvorhang
shower curtain

duschen
take a shower (v)

baden
take a bath (v)

die Zahnpflege • dental hygiene

die Zahnbürste
toothbrush

die
Zahnseide
dental floss

die Zahnpasta
toothpaste

das Mundwasser
mouthwash

der
Luffaschwamm
loofah

der Schwamm
sponge

der Bimsstein
pumice stone

die Rückenbürste
back brush

das Deo
deodorant

die
Seifenschale
soap dish

das **Duschgel**
shower gel

die Seife
soap

die Gesichtscreme
face cream

das Schaumbad
bubble bath

das Handtuch
hand towel

das
Badetuch
bath towel

die Handtücher
towels

die Körperlotion
body lotion

der Körperpuder
talcum powder

der Bademantel
bathrobe

das Rasieren • shaving

der
Elektrorasierer
electric razor

der Rasierschaum
shaving foam

die
Rasierklinge
razor blade

der Einwegrasierer
disposable razor

das Rasierwasser
aftershave

das Kinderzimmer • nursery

die Säuglingspflege • baby care

die Wundsalbe
diaper rash cream

das
Erfrischungstuch
wet wipe

der
Schwamm
sponge

die Babywanne
baby bath

das Töpfchen
potty

die Wickelmatte
changing mat

das Schlafen • sleeping

das Laken
sheet

die Decke
blanket

das Mobile
mobile

die Gitterstäbe
bars

die Flauschdecke
fleece

das Bettzeug
bedding

der Kopfschutz
bumper

die Matratze
mattress

das Kinderbett | crib

die Rassel
rattle

das Körbchen
bassinet

das Spielen • playing

die Puppe
doll

das Kuscheltier
soft toy

das Puppenhaus
dollhouse

das Spielhaus
playhouse

die Sicherheit • safety

die Kindersicherung
child lock

die Babysprechanlage
baby monitor

der Teddy
teddy bear

das Spielzeug
toy

der Spielzeugkorb
toy basket

der Ball
ball

der Laufstall
playpen

das Treppengitter
stair gate

das Essen • eating

der Kinderstuhl
high chair

der Sauger
teat

der Babybecher
drinking cup

die Babyflasche
bottle

das Ausgehen • going out

der Sportwagen
stroller

das Verdeck
hood

der Kinderwagen
baby carriage

der Kinderwagen
baby carriage

das Tragebettchen
carrier

die Windel
diaper

die Babytasche
diaper bag

die Babytrageschlinge
baby sling

der Allzweckraum • utility room

die Wäsche • laundry

die saubere Wäsche
clean clothes

die
schmutzige
Wäsche
dirty laundry

der Wäschekorb
laundry basket

**die
Waschmaschine**
washing machine

**der
Waschtrockner**
washer-dryer

der Trockner
tumble dryer

**der
Wäschekorb**
linen basket

die Wäscheleine
clothesline

das Bügeleisen
iron

die Wäsche
klammer
clothespin

trocknen
dry (v)

das Bügelbrett | ironing board

Vokabular • vocabulary

füllen load (v)	**schleudern** spin (v)	**bügeln** iron (v)	**Wie benutze ich die Waschmaschine?** How do I operate the washing machine?
spülen rinse (v)	**die Wäscheschleuder** spin-dryer	**der Weichspüler** fabric softener	**Welches Programm nehme ich für farbige/weiße Wäsche?** What is the setting for colors/whites?

die Reinigungsartikel • cleaning equipment

der Saugschlauch
suction hose

der Handfeger
brush

die Müllschaufel
dust pan

das Reinigungsmittel
bleach

der Eimer
pail

das Pulver
powder

die Flüssigkeit
liquid

das Staubtuch
duster

der Staubsauger
vacuum cleaner

der Mopp
mop

das Waschmittel
detergent

die Politur
polish

die Tätigkeiten • activities

putzen
clean (v)

spülen
wash (v)

wischen
wipe (v)

schrubben
scrub (v)

kratzen
scrape (v)

der Besen
broom

fegen
sweep (v)

Staub wischen
dust (v)

polieren
polish (v)

die Heimwerkstatt • workshop

das Bohrfutter
chuck

der Bohrer
drill bit

die Batterie
battery pack

die Stichsäge
jigsaw

der Bohrer mit Batteriebetrieb
cordless drill

der Elektrobohrer
electric drill

die Leimpistole
glue gun

die Zwinge
clamp

das Blatt
blade

der Schraubstock
vise

die Schleifmaschine
sander

die Kreissäge
circular saw

die Werkbank
workbench

der Holzleim
wood glue

das Werkzeuggestell
tool rack

der Grundhobel
router

die Bohrwinde
bit brace

die Holzspäne
wood shavings

die Verlängerungsschnur
extension cord

die Fertigkeiten • techniques

schneiden
cut (v)

sägen
saw (v)

bohren
drill (v)

hämmern
hammer (v)

der Lötzinn
solder

hobeln
plane (v)

drechseln
turn (v)

schnitzen
carve (v)

löten
solder (v)

die Materialien • materials

die MDF-Platte
MDF

das Sperrholz
plywood

das Spanholz
chipboard

die Hartfaserplatte
hardboard

das Weichholz
softwood

das Holz | wood

das Hartholz
hardwood

der Lack
varnish

die Beize
woodstain

der Draht
wire

das Kabel
cable

der rostfreie Stahl
stainless steel

galvanisiert
galvanized

das Metall | metal

der Werkzeugkasten • toolbox

der
Schrauben
schlüssel
wrench

der verstellbare
Schraubenschlüssel
adjustable wrench

der Hammer
hammer

die Flachzange
needlenose pliers

der Steckschlüssel
socket wrench

die
Schrauben
ziehereinsätze
screwdriver
bits

die
Wasserwaage
level

der
Dichtungsring
washer

der
Schraubenzieher
screwdriver

die Mutter
nut

das Metermaß
tape measure

der Schneider
knife

die Kombinationszange
bullnose pliers

die Tülle
socket

der Schlüssel
Allen key

---

die Bohrer • drill bits

der Metallbohrer
metal bit

der Flachholzbohrer
flat wood bit

der
Kreuzschlitzschraubenzieher
Phillips screwdriver

die Reibahle
reamer

der Nagelkopf
head

der
Sicherheits
bohrer
security bit

der Nagel
nail

die
Holzbohrer
carpentry bits

der
Mauerwerk-
bohrer
masonry bit

die Schraube
screw

---

die Entisolierzange
wire strippers

der Drahtschneider
wire cutters

der Lötkolben
soldering iron

das
Isolierband
insulating
tape

das
Skalpell
craft knife

die Schweifsäge
fretsaw

der Lötzinn
solder

die Profilsäge | tenon saw

die Schutzbrille
safety goggles

der Hobel
plane

die Gehrungslade
miter block

der Fuchsschwanz
handsaw

der Handbohrer
hand drill

die Stahlwolle
steel wool

die Metallsäge
hacksaw

der Meißel
chisel

das Schmirgelpapier
sandpaper

die Rohrzange
wrench

die Feile
file

der Wetzstahl
whetstone

der Sauger
plunger

der Rohrabschneider | pipe cutter

das Tapezieren • decorating

die Tapezierschere
scissors

das Tapeziermesser
utility knife

das Senkblei
plumb line

der Spachtel
scraper

der
Tapezierer
decorator

die Tapete
wallpaper

die Trittleiter
stepladder

die
Tapezierbürste
wallpaper brush

der
Tapeziertisch
pasting table

die
Kleisterbürste
pasting brush

der
Tapetenkleister
wallpaper paste

der Eimer
pail

tapezieren | wallpaper (v)

abziehen
strip (v)

spachteln
fill (v)

schmirgeln
sand (v)

verputzen | plaster (v)

anbringen | hang (v)

kacheln | tile (v)

der Roller
roller

die Streichbürste
brush

die Wanne
paint tray

die Farbe
paint

der Farbtopf
paint can

der Schwamm
sponge

das Abdeckband
masking tape

das Schmirgel papier
sandpaper

der Overall
overalls

das Abdecktuch
dustsheet

das Terpentin
turpentine

die Spachtelmasse
filler

das Verdünnungsmittel
mineral spirits

anstreichen
paint (v)

Vokabular • vocabulary

der Gips plaster	**Glanz-** gloss	**das Relieftapete** embossed paper	**die Grundierung** undercoat	**das Lösungsmittel** solvent
der Lack varnish	**matt** mat	**die Grundfarbe** primer	**der Fugenkitt** grout	**der Deckanstrich** topcoat
die Emulsionsfarbe latex paint	**die Schablone** stencil	**das Einsatzpapier** lining paper	**der Schutzanstrich** preservative	**das Versiegelungsmittel** sealant

der Garten • garden

die Gartentypen • garden styles

der Patio
patio garden

der architektonische Garten | formal garden

der Bauerngarten
cottage garden

der Kräutergarten
herb garden

der Dachgarten
roof garden

der Steingarten
rock garden

der Hof
courtyard

der Wassergarten
water garden

die Garten ornamente • garden features

die Blumenampel
hanging basket

das Spalier
trellis

die Pergola
pergola

die Platten
paving

der Weg
path

der Kompost
haufen
compost heap

das Tor
gate

das
Blumenbeet
flowerbed

der Boden
• soil

die Erde
topsoil

der Sand
sand

der Kalk
chalk

der Rasen
lawn

der Teich
pond

die Hecke
hedge

der Bogen
arch

der
Schuppen
shed

das
Gewächshaus
greenhouse

der Zaun
fence

der
Gemüsegarten
vegetable
garden

die Staudenrabatte
herbaceous border

der Schlick
silt

die Planken
decking

der Springbrunnen | fountain

der Lehm
clay

die Gartenpflanzen • garden plants

die Pflanzenarten • types of plants

einjährig
annual

zweijährig
biennial

mehrjährig
perennial

die Zwiebel
bulb

der Farn
fern

die Binse
rush

der Bambus
bamboo

das Unkraut
weeds

das Kraut
herb

die Wasserpflanze
water plant

der Baum
tree

die Palme
palm

der Nadelbaum
conifer

immergrün
evergreen

der Laubbaum
deciduous

86

der Formschnitt
topiary

die Alpenpflanze
alpine

die Fettpflanze
succulent

der Kaktus
cactus

die Topfpflanze
potted plant

die Schattenpflanze
shade plant

die Kletterpflanze
climber

der Zierstrauch
flowering shrub

der Bodendecker
ground cover

die Kriechpflanze
creeper

Zier-
ornamental

das Gras
grass

die Gartengeräte • garden tools

die Komposterde
compost

die Samen
seeds

die Knochenasche
bone meal

der Kies
gravel

der Laubrechen
lawn rake

der Spaten
spade

die Gabel
fork

die Schere
long-handled shears

der Rechen
rake

die Hacke
hoe

der Grasfangsack
grass bag

der Motor
motor

der Griff
handle

der Gartenkorb
trug

der Schutz
shield

der Ständer
stand

der Schneider
trimmer

der Rasenmäher
lawnmower

der Schubkarren
wheelbarrow

die Handgabel
hand fork

die Pflanzschaufel
trowel

das Messer
blade

die Heckenschere
shears

die Handsäge
hand saw

die Rosenschere
pruners

der Setzkasten
seed tray

das Pestizid
pesticide

die Gartenhandschuhe
gardening gloves

der Zwirn
twine

die Gartenstöcke
canes

das Sieb
sieve

der Blumentopf
plant pot

die Pflanzenschildchen
labels

die Befestigungen
twist ties

die Ringbefestigungen
ring ties

die Gummistiefel
rubber boots

das Gießen • watering

die Gartenspritze
spray bottle

die Gießkanne
watering can

die Brause
rose

der Rasensprenger
sprinkler

der Gartenschlauch
hose

die Düse
nozzle

der Schlauchwagen | hose reel

die Gartenarbeit • gardening

der Rasen
lawn

die Hecke
hedge

das
Blumenbeet
flowerbed

der
Rasenmäher
lawnmower

die Stange
stake

mähen | mow (v)

mit Rasen bedecken
turf (v)

stechen
spike (v)

harken
rake (v)

stutzen
trim (v)

graben
dig (v)

säen
sow (v)

**mit Kopfdünger
düngen**
topdress (v)

gießen
water (v)

deutsch • english

der Stock
cane

ziehen
train (v)

köpfen
deadhead (v)

sprühen
spray (v)

der Ableger
cutting

pfropfen
graft (v)

vermehren
propagate (v)

beschneiden
prune (v)

hochbinden
stake (v)

umpflanzen
transplant (v)

jäten
weed (v)

mulchen
mulch (v)

ernten
harvest (v)

Vokabular • vocabulary

züchten cultivate (v)	**gestalten** landscape (v)	**düngen** fertilize (v)	**sieben** sift (v)	**biodynamisch** organic	**die Entwässerung** drainage	**der Dünger** fertilizer
hegen tend (v)	**eintopfen** pot (v)	**pflücken** pick (v)	**auflockern** aerate (v)	**der Untergrund** subsoil	**der Unkrautvernichter** weedkiller	**der Sämling** seedling

die Dienstleistungen
services

die Dienstleistungen • emergency services

die Notdienste • ambulance

der Krankenwagen
ambulance

die Tragbahre
stretcher

der Rettungssanitäter
paramedic

die Polizei • police

die
Kenn-
marke
badge

die Uniform
uniform

die Sirene
siren

das Licht
lights

das Polizeiauto
police car

die Polizeiwache
police station

der
Gummiknüppel
nightstick

die
Pistole
gun

die
Handschellen
handcuffs

der Polizist
police officer

Vokabular • vocabulary

der Inspektor inspector	**das Verbrechen** crime	**die Beschwerde** complaint	**die Festnahme** arrest
der Kriminal-beamte detective	**der Einbruch-diebstahl** burglary	**die Ermittlung** investigation	**die Anklage** charge
die Polizeizelle cell	**die Körperve-rletzung** assault	**der Verdächtige** suspect	**der Finger abdruck** fingerprint

die Feuerwehr • fire department

der Schutzhelm
helmet

der Rauch
smoke

der Schlauch
hose

der
Auslegerkorb
basket

die Feuerwehrleute
firefighters

der
Wasserstrahl
water jet

die
Fahrer-
kabine
cab

die Leiter
ladder

der
Ausleger
boom

der Brand | fire

die Feuerwache
fire station

die Feuertreppe
fire escape

das Löschfahrzeug
fire engine

der Rauchmelder
smoke alarm

der Feuermelder
fire alarm

das Beil
ax

der
Feuerlöscher
fire extinguisher

der Hydrant
hydrant

Die Polizei/die Feuerwehr/einen Krankenwagen, bitte. I need the police/fire department/ambulance.	**Es brennt in…** There's a fire at…	**Es ist ein Unfall passiert.** There's been an accident.	**Rufen Sie die Polizei!** Call the police!

die Bank • bank

der Kunde
customer

der Schalter
window

der Kassierer
teller

die Broschüren
brochures

der Schalter
counter

**die Einzahlungs
scheine**
deposit slips

die EC-Karte
debit card

**der
Abschnitt**
stub

**die
Kontonummer**
account number

**die
Unterschrift**
signature

der Betrag
amount

der Filialleiter
bank manager

die Kreditkarte
credit card

das Scheckheft
checkbook

der Scheck
check

Vokabular • vocabulary

die Steuer tax	**die Hypothek** mortgage	**die Zahlung** payment	**einzahlen** deposit (v)	**das Girokonto** checking account
das Darlehen loan	**der Zinssatz** interest rate	**der Einzugsauftrag** automatic payment	**die Bankgebühr** bank charge	**das Sparkonto** savings account
die Spareinlagen savings	**die Kontoüberziehung** overdraft	**das Abhebungsformular** withdrawal slip	**die Banküberweisung** electronic transfer	**der PIN-Kode** PIN

die Münze
coin

der Schein
bill

der
Bildschirm
screen

das
Tastenfeld
key pad

der
Kartenschlitz
card slot

das Geld
money

der Geldautomat
ATM

---

die Währung • currency

die Wechselstube
bureau de change

der Reisescheck
traveler's check

der Wechselkurs
exchange rate

---

die Geldwirtschaft • finance

der Aktienpreis
share price

der
Börsenmakler
stockbroker

die Finanzberaterin
financial advisor

die Börse | stock exchange

Vokabular • vocabulary

einlösen cash (v)	**die Aktien** shares
der Nennwert denomination	**die Gewinnanteile** dividends
die Provision commission	**das Portefeuille** portfolio
die Wertpapiere stocks	**die Stammaktie** equity
die Kapitalanlage investment	**der Wirtschaftsprüfer** accountant
die ausländische Währung foreign currency	

Könnte ich das bitte wechseln?
Can I change this, please?

Wie ist der heutige Wechselkurs?
What's today's exchange rate?

---

die Kommunikation • communications

der Postbeamte
postal worker

der Schalter
window

die Waage
scale

der Schalter
counter

die Post | post office

der Poststempel
postmark

die Briefmarke
stamp

die Postleitzahl
ZIPcode

die Adresse
address

der Umschlag | envelope

der Briefträger
mail carrier

Vokabular • vocabulary

der Brief letter	**der Absender** return address	**die Zustellung** delivery	**zerbrechlich** fragile	**nicht falten** do not bend (v)
per Luftpost by airmail	**die Unterschrift** signature	**die Postgebühr** postage	**der Postsack** mailbag	**oben** this way up
das Einschreiben registered mail	**die Leerung** pickup	**die Postanweisung** money order	**das Telegramm** telegram	**das Fax** fax

---

deutsch • english

der Briefkasten
mailbox

der Hausbriefkasten
letter slot

das Paket
package

der Kurierdienst
courier

das Telefon • telephone

der Hörer
handset

die Basis
base station

der Anrufbeantworter
answering machine

das schnurlose Telefon
cordless phone

das Fernsehtelefon
video phone

die Telefonzelle
telephone booth

das Tastenfeld
keypad

der Hörer
receiver

die Münzrückgabe
coin return

das Handy
cell phone

der Münzfernsprecher
coin phone

das Kartentelefon
card phone

Vokabular • vocabulary

abheben answer (v)	**die Auskunft** directory assistance	**besetzt** busy	**Können Sie mir die Nummer für...geben?** Can you give me the number for...?
wählen dial (v)	**die SMS** text message	**unterbrochen** disconnected	**Was ist die Vorwahl für...?** What is the area code for...?
das R-Gespräch collect call	**die Sprachmitteilung** voice message	**die Vermittlung** operator	

---

das Hotel • hotel
die Empfangshalle • lobby

der Gast
guest

der Zimmerschlüssel
room key

die Nachrichten
messages

das Fach
pigeonhole

die
Empfangsdame
receptionist

das
Gästebuch
register

der Schalter
counter

der Empfang | reception

das
Gepäck
luggage

der Kofferkuli
cart

der Hoteldiener
porter

der Fahrstuhl
elevator

die Zimmernummer
room number

die Zimmer • rooms

das Einzelzimmer
single room

das Doppelzimmer
double room

das Zweibettzimmer
twin room

**das
Privatbadezimmer**
private bathroom

die Dienstleistungen • services

das Frühstückstablett
breakfast tray

die Zimmerreinigung
maid service

der Wäschedienst
laundry service

der Zimmerservice | room service

die Minibar
mini bar

das Restaurant
restaurant

der Fitnessraum
gym

das Schwimmbad
swimming pool

Vokabular • vocabulary

die Vollpension
full board

die Halbpension
half-board

die Übernachtung mit Frühstück
bed and breakfast

Haben Sie ein Zimmer frei?
Do you have any vacancies?

Ich möchte ein Einzelzimmer.
I'd like a single room.

Ich habe ein Zimmer reserviert.
I have a reservation.

Ich möchte ein Zimmer für drei Nächte.
I'd like a room for three nights.

Was kostet das Zimmer pro Nacht?
What is the charge per night?

Wann muss ich das Zimmer räumen?
When do I have to check out?

der Einkauf
shopping

das Einkaufszentrum • shopping center

das Atrium
atrium

die zweite
Etage
third floor

das Schild
sign

die erste
Etage
second
floor

die Rolltreppe
escalator

der
Fahrstuhl
elevator

das
Erdgeschoss
ground floor

der Kunde
customer

Vokabular • vocabulary

die Kinderabteilung
children's department

der Kundendienst
customer services

die Anprobe
changing rooms

Was kostet das?
How much is this?

die Gepäckabteilung
luggage department

die Anzeigetafel
store directory

der Wickelraum
baby-changing facilities

**Kann ich das
umtauschen?**
May I exchange this?

die Schuhabteilung
shoe department

der Verkäufer
sales clerk

die Toiletten
restrooms

---

deutsch • english

das Kaufhaus • department store

die
Herrenbekleidung
menswear

die
Damenoberbekleidung
women's clothing

die Damenwäsche
lingerie

die Parfümerie
perfume

die Schönheitspflege
beauty

die Wäsche
linen

die Möbel
home furnishings

die Kurzwaren
notions

die Küchengeräte
kitchenware

das Porzellan
china

die Elektroartikel
electrical goods

die Lampen
lighting

die Sportartikel
sports

die Spielwaren
toys

die Schreibwaren
stationery

die Lebensmittelabteilung
food

der Supermarkt • supermarket

der Gang
aisle

das
Warenregal
shelf

das Laufband
conveyor belt

der Kassierer
checker

die
Angebote
specials

die Kasse | checkout

der Kunde
customer

die Kasse
cash
register

die
Einkaufstasche
shopping bag

die
Lebensmittel
groceries

der Henkel
handle

der Strichkode
bar code

der Einkaufswagen
cart

der Einkaufskorb
basket

der Scanner
scanner

die Backwaren
bakery

die Milchprodukte
dairy

die Getreideflocken
cereals

die Konserven
canned food

die Süßwaren
confectionery

das Gemüse
vegetables

das Obst
fruit

das Fleisch und das Geflügel
meat and poultry

der Fisch
fish

die Feinkost
deli

die Gefrierware
frozen food

die Fertiggerichte
convenience food

die Getränke
drinks

die Haushaltswaren
household products

die Toilettenartikel
toiletries

die Babyprodukte
baby products

die Elektroartikel
electrical goods

das Tierfutter
pet food

die Zeitschriften | magazines

die Apotheke • pharmacy

die Zahnpflege
dental care

die Monats-hygiene
feminine hygiene

die Deos
deodorants

die Vitamintabletten
vitamins

die Apotheke
pharmacy

der Apotheker
pharmacist

das Hustenmedikament
cough medicine

das Kräuterheilmittel
herbal remedies

die Hautpflege
skin care

die Sonnenschutzcreme
sunscreen

die After-Sun-Lotion
aftersun

der Sonnenblock
sunblock

das Insektenschutzmittel
insect repellent

das Reinigungstuch
wet wipe

das Papiertaschentuch
tissue

die Damenbinde
sanitary napkin

der Tampon
tampon

die Slipeinlage
panty liner

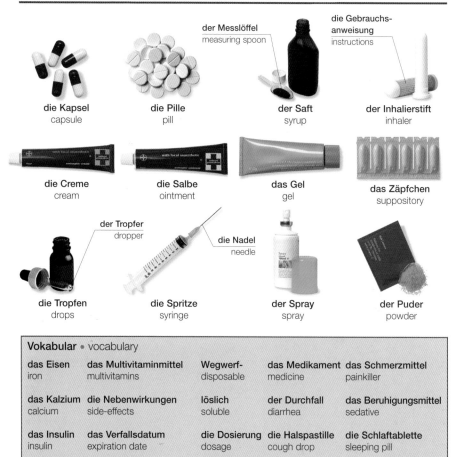

der Messlöffel
measuring spoon

die Gebrauchs- anweisung
instructions

die Kapsel
capsule

die Pille
pill

der Saft
syrup

der Inhalierstift
inhaler

die Creme
cream

die Salbe
ointment

das Gel
gel

das Zäpfchen
suppository

der Tropfer
dropper

die Nadel
needle

die Tropfen
drops

die Spritze
syringe

der Spray
spray

der Puder
powder

Vokabular • vocabulary

das Eisen iron	**das Multivitaminmittel** multivitamins	**Wegwerf-** disposable	**das Medikament** medicine	**das Schmerzmittel** painkiller
das Kalzium calcium	**die Nebenwirkungen** side-effects	**löslich** soluble	**der Durchfall** diarrhea	**das Beruhigungsmittel** sedative
das Insulin insulin	**das Verfallsdatum** expiration date	**die Dosierung** dosage	**die Halspastille** cough drop	**die Schlaftablette** sleeping pill
das Magnesium magnesium	**die Reisekrankheitstabletten** travel-sickness pills	**die Verordnung** medication	**das Abführmittel** laxative	**der Entzündungshemmer** anti-inflammatory

das Blumengeschäft • florist

die Blumen
flowers

die Lilie
lily

die Akazie
acacia

die Nelke
carnation

die Topfpflanze
potted plant

die Gladiole
gladiolus

die Iris
iris

die Margerite
daisy

die Chrysantheme
chrysanthemum

das Schleierkraut
gypsophila

die Levkoje
stocks

die Gerbera
gerbera

die Blätter
foliage

die Rose
rose

die Freesie
freesia

die
Blumenvase
vase

die Orchidee
orchid

die Pfingstrose
peony

der Strauß
bunch

der Stengel
stem

die Osterglocke
daffodil

die Knospe
bud

**das Ein
wickelpapier**
wrapping

die Tulpe | tulip

die Blumenarrangements • arrangements

das Band
ribbon

das Bukett
bouquet

die Trockenblumen
dried flowers

das Duftsträußchen | potpourri

der Kranz | wreath

die
Blumengirlande
garland

**Ich möchte einen Strauß...,
bitte.**
Can I have a bunch of...
please.

**Können Sie die Blumen
bitte einwickeln?**
Can I have them wrapped?

**Kann ich eine Nachricht
mitschicken?**
Can I attach a message?

Wie lange halten sie?
How long will these last?

Duften sie?
Are they fragrant?

**Können Sie die Blumen
an... schicken?**
Can you send them to....?

der Zeitungshändler • newsstand

die Zigaretten
cigarettes

das Päckchen Zigaretten
pack of cigarettes

die Streichhölzer
matches

die Lottoscheine
lottery tickets

die Briefmarken
stamps

die Postkarte
postcard

das Comicheft
comic

die Zeitschrift
magazine

die Zeitung
newspaper

das Rauchen • smoking

der Tabak
tobacco

das Feuerzeug
lighter

der Stiel
stem

der Kopf
bowl

die Pfeife
pipe

die Zigarre
cigar

der Konditor • confectionery

die Schachtel Pralinen
box of chocolates

die Nascherei
snack bar

die Chips
chips

das Süßwarengeschäft | candy store

Vokabular • vocabulary

die Milchschokolade milk chocolate	der Karamell caramel
die bittere Schokolade semisweet chocolate	der Trüffel truffle
	der Keks cookie
die weiße Schokolade white chocolate	die Bonbons hard candy
die bunte Mischung pick-and-mix	

die Süßwaren • confectionery

die Praline
chocolate

die Tafel Schokolade
chocolate bar

die Bonbons
candy

der Lutscher
lollipop

das Toffee
toffee

der Nugat
nougat

das Marshmallow
marshmallow

das Pfefferminz
mint

der Kaugummi
chewing gum

der Geleebonbon
jellybean

der Fruchtgummi
gumdrop

die Lakritze
licorice

andere Geschäfte • other stores

die Bäckerei
bread shop

die Konditorei
bakery

die Metzgerei
butcher shop

das Fischgeschäft
fish counter

der Gemüseladen
produce stand

**das
Lebensmittelgeschäft**
grocery store

das Schuhgeschäft
shoe store

**die Eisenwaren-
handlung**
hardware store

der Antiquitätenladen
antique shop

**der Geschenkartikel-
laden**
gift shop

das Reisebüro
travel agency

das Juweliergeschäft
jewelry store

der Buchladen
bookstore

das Plattengeschäft
record store

die Weinhandlung
liquor store

die Tierhandlung
pet store

das Möbelgeschäft
furniture store

die Boutique
boutique

Vokabular • vocabulary

das Gartencenter garden center	**das Fotogeschäft** camera store
die Reinigung dry-cleaner	**das Reformhaus** health-food store
der Waschsalon laundromat	**die Kunsthandlung** art store
der Immobilienmakler real estate office	**der Gebrauchtwarenhändler** second-hand store

die Schneiderei
tailor shop

der Frisiersalon
beauty salon

der Markt | market

die Nahrungsmittel
food

das Fleisch • meat

das
Lamm
lamb

der **Metzger**
butcher

der
Fleischerhaken
meat hook

die Waage
scale

der
Messerschärfer
knife sharpener

der Speck
bacon

die Würstchen
sausages

die Leber
liver

Vokabular • vocabulary

das Rindfleisch beef	**das Wild** venison	**die Zunge** tongue	**aus Freilandhaltung** free-range	**das rote Fleisch** red meat
das Kalbfleisch veal	**das Kaninchen** rabbit	**gepökelt** cured	**biologisch kontrolliert** organic	**das magere Fleisch** lean meat
das Schweinefleisch pork	**die Innereien** offal	**geräuchert** smoked	**das weiße Fleisch** white meat	**das gekochte Fleisch** cooked meat

---

die Fleischsorten • cuts

die Scheibe
slice

der Schinken
ham

die
Schwarte
rind

die Speckscheibe
bacon strip

das Hackfleisch
ground meat

das Filet
fillet

das Rumpsteak
rump steak

das Fett
fat

der
Knochen
bone

die Niere
kidney

das Lendensteak
sirloin steak

das Rippenstück
rib

das Kotelett
chop

die Keule
joint

das Herz
heart

das Geflügel • poultry

die Haut
skin

die Brust
breast

das Wild
game

das Bein
leg

der
Schenkel
thigh

das bratfertige
Huhn
dressed chicken

der Fasan | pheasant

die Wachtel | quail

der
Flügel
wing

die Pute
turkey

das Hähnchen | chicken

die Ente | duck

die Gans | goose

der Fisch • fish

die geschälten Garnelen
peeled shrimp

die rote Meeräsche
red mullet

die Heilbuttfilets
halibut fillets

die Regenbogenforelle
rainbow trout

das Eis
ice

die Rochenflügel
skate wings

das Fischgeschäft
fish counter

die Quappe
monkfish

die Makrele
mackerel

die Forelle
trout

der Schwertfisch
swordfish

die Seezunge
Dover sole

die Rotzunge
lemon sole

der Schellfisch
haddock

die Sardine
sardine

der Rochen
skate

der Weißfisch
whiting

der Seebarsch
sea bass

der Lachs | salmon

der Kabeljau
cod

der Seebrassen
sea bream

der Tunfisch
tuna

die Meeresfrüchte • seafood

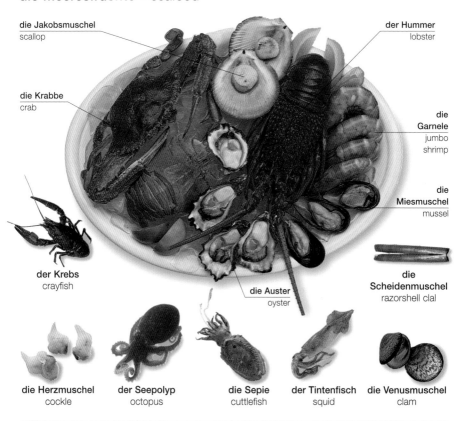

die Jakobsmuschel
scallop

der Hummer
lobster

die Krabbe
crab

die
Garnele
jumbo
shrimp

die
Miesmuschel
mussel

der Krebs
crayfish

die Auster
oyster

die
Scheidenmuschel
razorshell clal

die Herzmuschel
cockle

der Seepolyp
octopus

die Sepie
cuttlefish

der Tintenfisch
squid

die Venusmuschel
clam

Vokabular • vocabulary

tiefgefroren frozen	**gesalzen** salted	**zubereitet** cleaned	**entschuppt** descaled	**enthäutet** skinned	**die Lende** loin	**die Gräte** bone	**das Filet** fillet
frisch fresh	**geräuchert** smoked	**filetiert** filleted	**entgrätet** boned	**die Schuppe** scale	**der Schwanz** tail	**die Schnitte** steak	

---

das Gemüse 1 • vegetables 1

der Samen
seed

die dicke Bohne
fava bean

die Stangenbohne
green bean

die grüne Bohne
French bean

die grüne Erbse
garden pea

die Schote
pod

die
Sojabohnensprosse
bean sprout

der Bambus
bamboo

die Okra
okra

der Mais
corn

der Chicorée
chicory

der Fenchel
fennel

die Palmherzen
palm hearts

der
Stangensellerie
celery

Vokabular • vocabulary

das Blatt leaf	**das Röschen** floret	**die Spitze** tip	**biodynamisch** organic	**Verkaufen Sie Biogemüse?** Do you sell organic vegetables?
der Strunk stalk	**der Kern** kernel	**das Herz** heart	**die Plastiktüte** plastic bag	**Werden sie in dieser Gegend** **angebaut?** Are these grown locally?

die Rauke
arugula

die Brunnenkresse
watercress

der Radicchio
radicchio

der Rosenkohl
Brussels sprout

der Mangold
Swiss chard

der Grünkohl
kale

der Garten-Sauerampfer
sorrel

die Endivie
endive

der Löwenzahn
dandelion

der Spinat
spinach

der Kohlrabi
kohlrabi

der Chinakohl
pak-choi

der Salat
lettuce

der Brokkoli
broccoli

der Kohl
cabbage

der Frühkohl
spring greens

das Gemüse 2 • vegetables 2

die Artischocke
artichoke

das Radieschen
radish

der Blumenkohl
cauliflower

die Rübe
turnip

die
Kartoffel
potato

die
Zwiebel
onion

die Paprika
pepper

die Peperoni
chili pepper

der Gartenkürbis
marrow squash

Vokabular • vocabulary

die Kirschtomate cherry tomato	**der Sellerie** celeriac	**tiefgefroren** frozen	**bitter** bitter	**Könnte ich bitte ein Kilo Kartoffeln haben?** Can I have one kilo of potatoes, please?
die Karotte carrot	**die Tarowurzel** taro root	**roh** raw	**fest** firm	**Was kostet ein Kilo?** What's the price per kilo?
die Brotfrucht breadfruit	**der Maniok** cassava	**scharf** hot (spicy)	**das Fleisch** flesh	**Wie heißen diese?** What are those called?
die neue Kartoffel new potato	**die Wasserkastanie** water chestnut	**süß** sweet	**die Wurzel** root	

die Süßkartoffel
sweet potato

die Jamswurzel
yam

die Rote Bete
beet

die Kohlrübe
rutabaga

der Topinambur
Jerusalem
artichoke

der Meerrettich
horseradish

die Pastinake
parsnip

der Ingwer
ginger

die Aubergine
eggplant

die Tomate
tomato

**die
Frühlingszwiebel**
green onion

der Lauch
leek

die Schalotte
shallot

der Knoblauch
garlic

die Zehe
clove

die Trüffel
truffle

der Pilz
mushroom

die Gurke
cucumber

die Zucchini
zucchini

der Butternusskürbis
butternut squash

der Eichelkürbis
acorn squash

der Kürbis
pumpkin

das Obst 1 • fruit 1

die Zitrusfrüchte • citrus fruit

die Orange
orange

die Klementine
clementine

die weiße Haut
pith

die Tangelo
ugli fruit

die Grapefruit
grapefruit

der Schnitz
segment

die Satsuma
satsuma

die Mandarine
tangerine

die Schale
zest

die Limone
lime

die Zitrone
lemon

die Kumquat
kumquat

das Steinobst • stone fruit

der Pfirsich
peach

die Nektarine
nectarine

die Aprikose
apricot

die Pflaume
plum

die Kirsche
cherry

der Apfel
apple

die Birne
pear

der Obstkorb | basket of fruit

das Beerenobst und die Melonen • berries and melons

die Erdbeere
strawberry

die Himbeere
raspberry

die Melone
melon

die Weintrauben
grapes

die Johannisbeere
red currant

die Schale
rind

die Brombeere
blackberry

**die schwarze
Johannisbeere**
black currant

der Kern
seed

**das
Fruchtfleisch**
flesh

die Preiselbeere
cranberry

die Heidelbeere
blueberry

die weiße Johannisbeere
white currant

die Wassermelone
watermelon

die Loganbeere
loganberry

die Stachelbeere
gooseberry

Vokabular • vocabulary

saftig juicy	**sauer** sour	**knackig** crisp	**kernlos** seedless	**Sind sie reif?** Are they ripe?
die Faser fiber	**frisch** fresh	**faul** rotten	**der Saft** juice	**Könnte ich eine probieren?** Can I try one?
süß sweet	**der Rhabarber** rhubarb	**das Fruchtmark** pulp	**das Kerngehäuse** core	**Wie lange halten sie sich?** How long will they keep?

das Obst 2 • fruit 2

die Mango
mango

die Avocado
avocado

die Ananas
pineapple

die Papaya
papaya

der Pfirsich
peach

die Litschi
lychee

die Kiwi
kiwifruit

die Kapstachelbeere
cape gooseberry

der Kern
seed

die Schale
skin

die Quitte
quince

die Passionsfrucht
passion fruit

die Banane
banana

die Guave
guava

der Granatapfel
pomegranate

die Kaki
persimmon

die Feijoa
feijoa

die Kaktusfeige
prickly pear

die Sternfrucht
starfruit

die Mangostane
mangosteen

die Nüsse und das Dörrobst • nuts and dried fruit

die Piniennuss
pine nut

die Pistazie
pistachio

die Cashewnuss
cashew

die Erdnuss
peanut

die Haselnuss
hazelnut

die Paranuss
Brazil nut

die Pecannuss
pecan

die Mandel
almond

die Walnuss
walnut

die Esskastanie
chestnut

die Schale
shell

die Macadamianuss
macadamia

die Feige
fig

die Dattel
date

die Backpflaume
prune

das
Fruchtfleisch
flesh

die Sultanine
sultana raisin

die Rosine
raisin

die Korinthe
currant

die Kokosnuss
coconut

Vokabular • vocabulary

grün green	**hart** hard	**der Kern** kernel	**gesalzen** salted	**geröstet** roasted	**die Südfrüchte** tropical fruit	**geschält** shelled
reif ripe	**weich** soft	**getrocknet** desiccated	**roh** raw	**Saison-** seasonal	**die kandierten Früchte** candied fruit	**ganz** whole

die Getreidearten und die Hülsenfrüchte •
grains and legumes

das Getreide • grains

der Weizen
wheat

der Hafer
oats

die Gerste
barley

die Hirse
millet

der Mais
corn

die Reismelde
quinoa

Vokabular • vocabulary		
trocken dry	frisch fresh	Vollkorn whole-grain
die Hülse husk	aromatisch fragranced	Langkorn long-grain
der Kern kernel	einweichen soak (v)	Rundkorn short-grain
der Samen seed	die Getreideflocken cereal	leicht zu kochen easy-cook

der Reis • rice

der weiße Reis
white rice

der Naturreis
brown rice

der Wasserreis
wild rice

der Milchreis
pudding rice

die verarbeiteten Getreidearten •
processed grains

der Kuskus
couscous

der Weizenschrot
cracked wheat

der Grieß
semolina

die Kleie
bran

die Bohnen und die Erbsen • beans and peas

die Mondbohnen
butter beans

die weißen Bohnen
haricot beans

die roten Bohnen
red kidney beans

die Adzuki-bohnen
aduki beans

die Saubohnen
fava beans

die Sojabohnen
soybeans

die Teparybohnen
black-eyed beans

die Pintobohnen
pinto beans

die Mungbohnen
mung beans

die französischen Bohnen
flageolet beans

die braunen Linsen
brown lentils

die roten Linsen
red lentils

die grünen Erbsen
green peas

die Kichererbsen
garbanzos

die getrockneten Erbsen
split peas

die Körner • seeds

der Kürbiskern
pumpkin seed

das Senfkorn
mustard seed

der Kümmel
caraway

das Sesamkorn
sesame seed

der Sonnenblumenkern
sunflower seed

die Kräuter und Gewürze • herbs and spices

die Gewürze • spices

die Vanille
vanilla

die Muskatnuss
nutmeg

die Muskatblüte
mace

die Kurkuma
turmeric

der Kreuzkümmel
cumin

die Kräutermischung
bouquet garni

der Piment
allspice

das Pfefferkorn
peppercorn

der Bockshornklee
fenugreek

der Chili
chili powder

ganz
whole

zerstoßen
crushed

der Safran
saffron

der Kardamom
cardamom

das Currypulver
curry powder

gemahlen
ground

der Paprika
paprika

geraspelt
flakes

der Knoblauch
garlic

die Kräuter • herbs

die Stangen
sticks

der Zimt
cinnamon

**das
Zitronengras**
lemon grass

die Gewürznelke
cloves

der Sternanis
star anise

der Ingwer
ginger

der Fenchel
fennel

**die
Fenchelsamen**
fennel seeds

der Schnittlauch
chives

der Estragon
tarragon

der Oregano
oregano

die Minze
mint

der Majoran
marjoram

der Koriander
cilantro

das Lorbeerblatt
bay leaf

der Thymian
thyme

das Basilikum
basil

der Dill
dill

die Petersilie
parsley

der Salbei
sage

der Rosmarin
rosemary

die Nahrungsmittel in Flaschen • bottled foods

der Korken
cork

das Sonnenblumenöl
sunflower oil

das Walnussöl
walnut oil

das Traubenkernöl
grapeseed oil

das Mandelöl
almond oil

das Sesamöl
sesame oil

das Haselnussöl
hazelnut oil

das Olivenöl
olive oil

die Kräuter
herbs

das aromatische Öl
flavored oil

die Öle
oils

der süße Aufstrich • sweet spreads

das Glas
jar

die Honigwabe
honeycomb

der feste Honig
candied honey

der Zitronenaufstrich
lemon curd

die Himbeerkonfitüre
raspberry jam

die Orangenmarmelade
marmalade

der flüssige Honig
clear honey

der Ahornsirup
maple syrup

die Würzen • condiments and spreads

die Flasche
bottle

**der
Apfelweinessig**
cider vinegar

**der
Gewürzessig**
balsamic vinegar

**der englische
Senf**
English mustard

die Majonäse
mayonnaise

der Ketchup
ketchup

**der französische
Senf**
French mustard

das Chutney
chutney

der Malzessig
malt vinegar

der Weinessig
wine vinegar

der Essig
vinegar

die Soße
sauce

der grobe Senf
whole-grain
mustard

---

das Einmachglas
sealed jar

**die
Erdnussbutter**
peanut butter

**der
Schokoladenaufstrich**
chocolate spread

**das eingemachte
Obst**
preserved fruit

Vokabular • vocabulary

das Pflanzenöl vegetable oil	**das Rapsöl** canola oil
das Maiskeimöl corn oil	**das kaltgepresste Öl** cold-pressed oil
das Erdnussöl peanut oil	

die Milchprodukte • dairy produce

der Käse • cheese

die Rinde
rind

der mittelharte Käse
semi-hard cheese

der geriebene Käse
grated cheese

der Hartkäse
hard cheese

der halbfeste Käse
semi-soft cheese

der Hüttenkäse
cottage cheese

der Rahmkäse
cream cheese

der Blauschimmelkäse
blue cheese

der Weichkäse
soft cheese

der Frischkäse | fresh cheese

die Milch • milk

die Vollmilch
whole milk

die Halbfettmilch
reduced-fat milk

die Magermilch
skim milk

die Milchtüte
milk carton

die Ziegenmilch
goat's milk

die Kondensmilch
condensed milk

die Kuhmilch | cow's milk

die Butter
butter

die Margarine
margarine

die Sahne
cream

die fettarme Sahne
light cream

die Schlagsahne
heavy cream

die Schlagsahne
whipped cream

die saure Sahne
sour cream

der Joghurt
yogurt

das Eis
ice cream

die Eier • eggs

das Eigelb
yolk

das Eiweiß
egg white

die Eierschale
shell

der Eier
becher
egg cup

das gekochte Ei
boiled egg

das Hühnerei
hen's egg

das Entenei
duck egg

das Gänseei
goose egg

das Wachtelei
quail egg

Vokabular • vocabulary

pasteurisiert pasteurized	**fettfrei** fat-free	**gesalzen** salted	**die Schafmilch** sheep's milk	**die Laktose** lactose	**der Milchshake** milkshake
unpasteurisiert unpasteurized	**das Milchpulver** powdered milk	**ungesalzen** unsalted	**die Buttermilch** buttermilk	**homogenisiert** homogenized	**der gefrorene Joghurt** frozen yogurt

das Brot und das Mehl • breads and flours

das Scheibenbrot
sliced bread

der Mohn
poppy seeds

das Roggenbrot
rye bread

das Baguette
baguette

die Bäckerei | bakery

Brot backen • making bread

das Weizenmehl
white flour

das Roggenmehl
brown flour

das Vollkornmehl
whole-wheat flour

die Hefe
yeast

sieben | sift (v)

verrühren | mix (v)

der Teig
dough

backen | bake (v)

die Kruste
crust

der Laib
loaf

die Scheibe
slice

das Weißbrot
white bread

das Graubrot
brown bread

das Vollkornbrot
whole-wheat bread

das Mehrkornbrot
multigrain bread

das Maisbrot
cornbread

das Sodabrot
soda bread

das Sauerteigbrot
sourdough bread

das Fladenbrot
flatbread

das Hefebrötchen
bagel

das weiche Brötchen
bun

das Brötchen
roll

das Rosinenbrot
fruit bread

das Körnerbrot
seeded bread

der Naan
naan bread

das Pitabrot
pita bread

das Knäckebrot
crispbread

Vokabular • vocabulary

das angereicherte Mehl bread flour	**das Paniermehl** breadcrumbs	**gehen lassen** prove (v)	**aufgehen** rise (v)	**der Brotschneider** slicer
das Mehl mit Backpulver self-rising flour	**das Mehl ohne Backpulver** all-purpose flour	**glasieren** glaze (v)	**die Flöte** flute	**der Bäcker** baker

Kuchen und Nachspeisen • cakes and desserts

das Eclair
éclair

der Brandteig
choux pastry

der Blätterteig
puff pastry

die Sahne
cream

der Blätterteig
phyllo pastry

die Füllung
filling

mit Schokolade überzogen
chocolate-coated

der englische Kuchen
fruit cake

das Obsttortelett
fruit tart

der Muffin
muffin

das Biskuittörtchen
sponge cake

das Baiser
meringue

das Gebäck | cakes

Vokabular • vocabulary

die Konditorcreme crème patisserie	**das Teilchen** bun	**der Teig** pastry	**der Milchreis** rice pudding	**Könnte ich bitte ein Stück haben?** May I have a slice, please?
die Schokoladentorte chocolate cake	**der Vanillepudding** custard	**das Stück** slice	**die Feier** celebration	

das Schokoladen-
stückchen
chocolate chip

die Löffelbiskuits
lady fingers

das Trifle
trifle

der Florentiner
florentine

die Kekse | cookies

die Mousse
mousse

das Sorbett
sherbet

die Sahnetorte
cream pie

der Karamellpudding
crème caramel

die festlichen Kuchen • celebration cakes

der obere Kuchenteil
top tier

das Band
ribbon

die
Dekoration
decoration

die
Geburtstagskerzen
birthday candles

ausblasen
blow out (v)

der untere
Kuchenteil
bottom tier

der
Zuckerguss
icing

das
Marzipan
marzipan

die Hochzeitstorte | wedding cake

der Geburtstagskuchen | birthday cake

die Feinkost • delicatessen

die pikante Wurst
spicy sausage

die Quiche
quiche

der Essig
vinegar

das Öl
oil

das frische Fleisch
uncooked meat

die Theke
counter

die Salami
salami

die Pepperoniwurst
pepperoni

die Pastete
pâté

der Mozzarella
mozzarella

der Brie
brie

der Ziegenkäse
goat's cheese

der Cheddar
cheddar

der Parmesan
parmesan

der Camembert
camembert

die Rinde
rind

der Edamer
edam

der Manchego
manchego

die Pasteten
meat pies

die schwarze Olive
black olive

die Peperoni
chili pepper

die Soße
sauce

das Brötchen
bread roll

das gekochte Fleisch
cooked meat

die grüne Olive
green olive

der Schinken
ham

die Sandwichtheke
sandwich counter

der Räucherfisch
smoked fish

die Kapern
capers

die Chorizo
chorizo

der Prosciutto
prosciutto

die gefüllte Olive
stuffed olive

Vokabular • vocabulary

in Öl	**mariniert**	**geräuchert**
in oil	marinated	smoked
in Lake	**gepökelt**	**getrocknet**
in brine	salted	cured

Nehmen Sie bitte eine Nummer.
Take a number, please.

Kann ich bitte etwas davon probieren?
Can I try some of that, please?

Ich hätte gerne sechs Scheiben davon, bitte.
May I have six slices of that, please?

die Getränke • drinks

das Wasser • water

die heißen Getränke • hot drinks

das Flaschenwasser
bottled water

mit Kohlensäure
sparkling

das Leitungswasser
tap water

ohne Kohlensäure
still

das Tonicwater
tonic water

das Sodawasser
soda water

das Mineralwasser
mineral water

der Teebeutel
tea bag

die Teeblätter
loose tea

der Tee
tea

die Bohnen
beans

der gemahlene Kaffee
ground coffee

der Kaffee
coffee

die heiße Schokolade
hot chocolate

das Malzgetränk
malted drink

die alkoholfreien Getränke • soft drinks

der Strohhalm
straw

der Tomatensaft
tomato juice

der Traubensaft
grape juice

die Limonade
lemonade

die Orangeade
orangeade

die Cola
cola

die alkoholischen Getränke • alcoholic drinks

die Dose
can

das Bier
beer

der Apfelwein
cider

das halbdunkle Bier
bitter

der Stout
stout

der Gin
gin

der Wodka
vodka

der Whisky
whiskey

der Rum
rum

der Weinbrand
brandy

trocken
dry

rosé
rosé

weiß
white

rot
red

der Portwein
port

der Sherry
sherry

der Campari
campari

der Likör
liqueur

der Tequila
tequila

der Champagner
champagne

der Wein
wine

auswärts essen
eating out

das Café • café

der
Sonnenschirm
umbrella

die **Markise**
awning

die
Speisekarte
menu

das Terrassencafé
terrace café

der
Kellner   die **Kaffeemaschine**   der **Tisch**
waiter   coffee machine   table

das Straßencafé | sidewalk café

die Snackbar | snack bar

der Kaffee • coffee

der **Kaffee mit Milch**
coffee with milk

der **schwarze**   das
Kaffee   **Kakaopulver**
black coffee   cocoa powder

der **Schaum**
froth

der Filterkaffee
filter coffee

der Espresso
espresso

der Cappuccino
cappuccino

der Eiskaffee
iced coffee

der Tee • tea

der Kräutertee
herbal tea

der Kamillentee
chamomile tea

der grüne Tee
green tea

der Tee mit Milch
tea with milk

der schwarze Tee
black tea

der Tee mit Zitrone
tea with lemon

der Pfefferminztee
mint tea

der Eistee
iced tea

die Säfte und Milchshakes • juices and milkshakes

der Schokoladenmilchshake
chocolate milkshake

der Erdbeermilchshake
strawberry milkshake

der Orangensaft
orange juice

der Apfelsaft
apple juice

der Ananassaft
pineapple juice

der Tomatensaft
tomato juice

der Kaffeemilchshake
coffee milkshake

das Essen • food

das Graubrot
whole-wheat bread

die Kugel
scoop

der getoastete Sandwich
toasted sandwich

der Salat
salad

das Eis
ice cream

das Gebäck
pastry

die Bar • bar

die Gläser
glasses

das Maß
optic

die Kasse
cash register

der Barkeeper
bartender

der Zapfhahn
beer tap

die Kaffeemaschine
coffee machine

der Eiskübel
ice bucket

der Barhocker
bar stool

der Aschbecher
ashtray

der Untersetzer
coaster

die Theke
bar counter

der Flaschenöffner
bottle opener

der Hebel
lever

die Eiszange
tongs

der Cocktailrührer
stirrer

der Messbecher
measure

der Korkenzieher | corkscrew

der Cocktailshaker | cocktail shaker

der Krug
pitcher

der Eiswürfel
ice cube

der Gin Tonic
gin and tonic

der Scotch mit Wasser
scotch and water

der Rum mit Cola
rum and cola

der Wodka mit Orangensaft
screwdriver

der Martini
martini

der Cocktail
cocktail

der Wein
wine

das Bier | beer

einfach
single

doppelt
double

Eis und Zitrone
ice and lemon

ein Schuss
shot

das Maß
measure

ohne Eis
without ice

mit Eis
with ice

die Knabbereien • bar snacks

die Cashewnüsse
cashews

die Erdnüsse
peanuts

die Mandeln
almonds

die Kartoffelchips | chips

die Nüsse | nuts

die Oliven | olives

das Restaurant • restaurant

der Nicht-raucherbereich
nonsmoking section

die Serviette
napkin

der Hilfskoch
commis chef

das Gedeck
table setting

der Küchenchef
chef

die Küche
kitchen

das Glas
glass

das Tablett
tray

der Kellner
waiter

Vokabular • vocabulary

das Abendmenü evening menu	**die Spezialitäten** specials	**der Preis** price	**das Trinkgeld** tip	**das Buffet** buffet	**der Kunde** customer
die Weinkarte wine list	**à la carte** à la carte	**die Quittung** receipt	**ohne Bedienung** service not included	**die Bar** bar	**das Salz** salt
das Mittagsmenü lunch menu	**der Dessertwagen** dessert cart	**die Rechnung** check	**Bedienung inbegriffen** service included	**der Raucherbereich** smoking section	**der Pfeffer** pepper

---

die Speisekarte
menu

die Kinderportion
child's meal

bestellen
order (v)

bezahlen
pay (v)

die Gänge • courses

der Aperitif
apéritif

die Vorspeise
appetizer

die Suppe
soup

das Hauptgericht
entrée

die Beilage
side order

die Gabel
fork

der Kaffeelöffel
coffee spoon

der Nachtisch | dessert

der Kaffee | coffee

Ein Tisch für zwei Personen bitte.
A table for two, please.

Könnte ich bitte die Speisekarte/Weinliste sehen?
Can I see the menu/winelist, please?

Gibt es ein Festpreismenü?
Is there a fixed-price menu?

Haben Sie vegetarische Gerichte?
Do you have any vegetarian dishes?

Könnte ich die Rechnung/Quittung haben?
Could I have the check/a receipt, please?

Könnten wir getrennt zahlen?
Can we pay separately?

Wo sind die Toiletten bitte ?
Where are the restrooms, please?

der Schnellimbiss • fast food

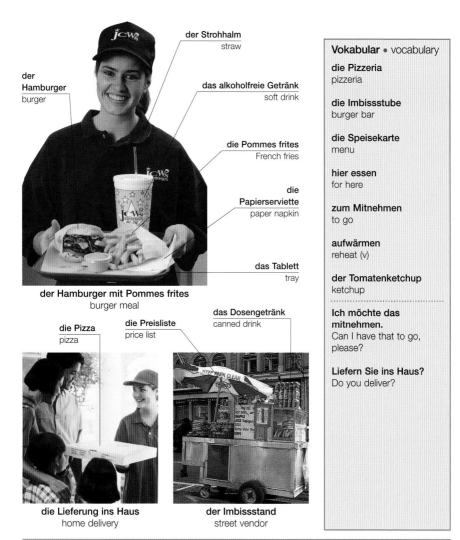

der Strohhalm
straw

der Hamburger
burger

das alkoholfreie Getränk
soft drink

die Pommes frites
French fries

die Papierserviette
paper napkin

das Tablett
tray

der Hamburger mit Pommes frites
burger meal

die Pizza
pizza

die Preisliste
price list

das Dosengetränk
canned drink

die Lieferung ins Haus
home delivery

der Imbissstand
street vendor

Vokabular • vocabulary

die Pizzeria
pizzeria

die Imbissstube
burger bar

die Speisekarte
menu

hier essen
for here

zum Mitnehmen
to go

aufwärmen
reheat (v)

der Tomatenketchup
ketchup

Ich möchte das mitnehmen.
Can I have that to go, please?

Liefern Sie ins Haus?
Do you deliver?

das Brötchen bun

der Senf mustard

die Wurst sausage

der Hamburger hamburger

der Chickenburger chicken burger

der vegetarische Hamburger veggie burger

das Hot Dog hot dog

die Füllung filling

der Sandwich sandwich

der Klubsandwich club sandwich

das belegte Brot open-face sandwich

das gefüllte Fladenbrot wrap

die Soße sauce

salzig savory

süß sweet

der Pizzabelag topping

der Kebab kebab

die Hähnchenstückchen chicken nuggets

die Crêpes | crêpes

der Bratfisch mit Pommes frites fish and chips

die Rippen ribs

das gebratene Hähnchen fried chicken

die Pizza pizza

das Frühstück • breakfast

die Milch
milk

die Getreide flocken
cereal

die Konfitüre
jam

das Dörrobst
dried fruit

der Schinken
ham

der Käse
cheese

das Knäckebrot
crispbread

das Frühstücksbuffet
breakfast buffet

die Orangenmarmelade
marmalade

die Pastete
pâté

die Butter
butter

der Obstsaft
fruit juice

der Kaffee
coffee

die Schokolade
hot chocolate

das Croissant
croissant

der Tee
tea

der Frühstückstisch | breakfast table

die Getränke | drinks

die Tomate
tomato

die Blutwurst
black pudding

der Toast
toast

das
Würstchen
sausage

das Spiegelei
fried egg

der Frühstücks
speck
bacon

die Brioche
brioche

das Brot
bread

das englische Frühstück
English breakfast

das Eigelb
yolk

die Räucherheringe
kippers

das in Ei gebratene Brot
French toast

das gekochte Ei
boiled egg

das Rührei
scrambled eggs

die Sahne
cream

der Früchtejoghurt
fruit yogurt

die Pfannkuchen
crêpes

die Waffeln
waffles

der Porridge
oatmeal

das Obst
fresh fruit

die Hauptmahlzeit • dinner

die Suppe | soup

die Brühe | broth

der Eintopf | stew

das Curry | curry

der Braten
roast

die Pastete
pie

das Soufflé
soufflé

der Schaschlik
kebab

die Fleischklöße
meatballs

das Omelett
omelet

das Schnellbratgericht
stir-fry

die Nudeln
noodles

die Nudeln | pasta

der Reis
rice

der gemischte Salat
tossed salad

der grüne Salat
green salad

die Salatsoße
dressing

die Zubereitung • techniques

gefüllt | stuffed **in Soße** | in sauce **gegrillt** | grilled **mariniert** | marinated

pochiert | poached **püriert** | mashed **gebacken** | baked **kurzgebraten** | pan-fried

gebraten
fried **eingelegt**
pickled **geräuchert**
smoked **frittiert**
deep-fried

in Saft
in syrup **angemacht**
dressed **gedämpft**
steamed **getrocknet**
cured

das Lernen
study

die Schule • school

die Lehrerin
teacher

die Tafel
blackboard

der Schuljunge
schoolboy

der Schüler
student

die
Schuluniform
school uniform

das Pult
desk

die Schultasche
schoolbag

die Kreide
chalk

das Klassenzimmer | classroom

das Schulmädchen
schoolgirl

Vokabular • vocabulary

die Literatur literature	die Kunst art	die Physik physics
die Sprachen languages	die Musik music	die Chemie chemistry
die Erdkunde geography	die Mathematik math	die Biologie biology
die Geschichte history	die Naturwiss- enschaft science	der Sport physical education

die Aktivitäten • activities

lesen | read (v)

schreiben | write (v)

buchstabieren
spell (v)

zeichnen
draw (v)

die Feder
nib

der Buntstift
colored pencil

der Spitzer
pencil
sharpener

der Overheadprojektor
overhead projector

der Füller
pen

der Bleistift
pencil

der Radiergummi
eraser

das Heft
notebook

das Schulbuch | textbook

das Federmäppchen
pencil case

das Lineal
ruler

fragen
question (v)

antworten
answer (v)

diskutieren
discuss (v)

lernen
learn (v)

Vokabular • vocabulary

der Schulleiter principal	die Antwort answer	die Note grade
die Stunde lesson	der Aufsatz essay	die Klasse year
die Frage question	die Prüfung test	das Lexikon encyclopedia
Notizen machen take notes (v)	die Hausaufgabe homework	das Wörterbuch dictionary

die Mathematik • math

die Formen • shapes

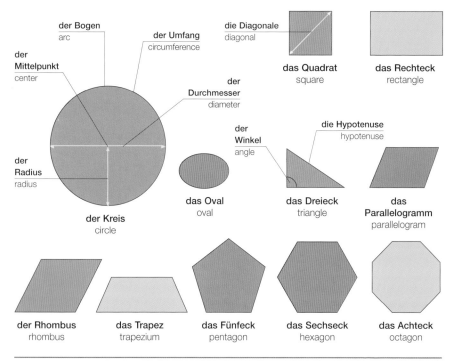

der Bogen
arc

der Umfang
circumference

die Diagonale
diagonal

der
Mittelpunkt
center

der
Durchmesser
diameter

das Quadrat
square

das Rechteck
rectangle

der
Winkel
angle

die Hypotenuse
hypotenuse

der
Radius
radius

das Oval
oval

das Dreieck
triangle

das
Parallelogramm
parallelogram

der Kreis
circle

der Rhombus
rhombus

das Trapez
trapezium

das Fünfeck
pentagon

das Sechseck
hexagon

das Achteck
octagon

die Körper • solids

die Seite
side

die Spitze
apex

die
Grundfläche
base

der Kegel
cone

der Zylinder
cylinder

der Würfel
cube

die Pyramide
pyramid

die Kugel
sphere

die Linien • lines

gerade	parallel	senkrecht	gekrümmt
straight	parallel	perpendicular	curved

die Maße • measurements

die Breite
width

die Länge
length

der Zähler
numerator

die Höhe
height

der Nenner
denominator

die Tiefe
depth

das Volumen	der Bruch	die Abmessungen	die Fläche
volume	fraction	dimensions	area

die Ausrüstung • equipment

das Zeichendreieck	der Winkelmesser	das Lineal	der Zirkel	der Taschenrechner
square	protractor	ruler	compass	calculator

Vokabular • vocabulary

die Geometrie	plus	mal	gleich	addieren	multiplizieren	die Gleichung
geometry	plus	times	equals	add (v)	multiply (v)	equation

die Arithmetik	minus	geteilt durch	zählen	subtrahieren	dividieren	der Prozentsatz
arithmetic	minus	divided by	count (v)	subtract (v)	divide (v)	percentage

die Wissenschaft • science

das Labor
laboratory

die Laborwaage
scales

das Gewicht
weight

die Federwaage
spring balance

der Tiegel
crucible

der Bunsenbrenner
bunsen burner

der Dreifuß
tripod

die Glasflasche
glass bottle

das Stativ
lamp stand

das Reagenzglas
test tube

das Gestell
rack

der Trichter
funnel

die Klammer
clamp

der Stöpsel
stopper

der Zeitmesser
timer

der Kolben
flask

die Petrischale
petri dish

der Versuch | experiment

das Thermometer
thermometer

die Spritze
syringe

die Pinzette
tweezers

das Skalpell
scalpel

der Tropfer
dropper

die Zange | forceps

die Greifzange
tongs

der Spatel
spatula

die Keule
pestle

das Okular
eyepiece

**der Einstell-
knopf**
focusing knob

der Mörser
mortar

das Filterpapier
filter paper

die Schutzbrille
safety goggles

das Glasstäbchen
glass stirrer

**die
Objektivlinse**
objective lens

der Tisch
stage

die Pipette
pipette

das Becherglas
beaker

der Objektträger
slide

der Magnet
magnet

die Krokodilklemme
alligator clip

der Spiegel
mirror

**die positive
Elektrode**
positive
electrode

die negative Elektrode
negative electrode

das Mikroskop | microscope

die Batterie | battery

die Hochschule • college

das Sekretariat
admissions office

der
Sportplatz
sports field

die Mensa
cafeteria

das Studenten-
heim
residence hall

die Gesundheits-
fürsorge
clinic

der Campus | campus

der Katalog
card catalog

die Bibliothekarin
librarian

Vokabular • vocabulary

der Leserausweis library card	**die Auskunft** helpdesk	**verlängern** renew (v)
der Lesesaal reading room	**ausleihen** borrow (v)	**das Buch** book
die Literaturliste reading list	**vorbestellen** reserve (v)	**der Titel** title
das Rückgabedatum due date	**die Ausleihe** loan	**der Gang** aisle

die Ausleihe
circulation desk

das
Bücher
regal
bookshelf

das
Periodikum
periodical

die
Zeitschrift
journal

die Bibliothek | library

der Student
undergraduate

der Dozent
professor

die Graduierte
graduate

die Robe
gown

der Hörsaal
lecture hall

die Graduierungsfeier
graduation ceremony

die Fachhochschulen • schools

das Model
model

die Kunsthochschule
art college

die Musikhochschule
music school

die Tanzakademie
dance academy

Vokabular • vocabulary

das Stipendium scholarship	die Forschung research	die Examensarbeit dissertation	die Medizin medicine	die Philosophie philosophy
postgraduiert postgraduate	der Magister master's	der Fachbereich department	die Zoologie zoology	die Politologie politics
das Diplom diploma	die Promotion doctorate	der Maschinenbau engineering	die Physik physics	die Literatur literature
der akademische Grad degree	die Dissertation thesis	die Kunstgeschichte art history	die Rechtswissenschaft law	
			die Wirtschaftswissenschaft economics	

die Arbeit
work

das Büro 1 • office 1
das Büro • office

der Bildschirm
monitor

der Stifthalter
desktop organizer

der Ordner
file

die Ablage für Eingänge
in-tray

die Ablage
für Ausgänge
out-tray

der Computer
computer

die Tastatur
keyboard

das Telefon
telephone

das
Notizbuch
notebook

das Schild
label

der
Schreibtisch
desk

der
Papierkorb
wastebasket

der Drehstuhl
swivel chair

das
Schreibtischschränkchen
drawer unit

die
Schublade
drawer

der Aktenschrank
filing cabinet

die Büroausstattung • office equipment

der
Papierbehälter
paper tray

die
Papierführung
paper guide

das Fax
fax

der Drucker | printer

das Faxgerät | fax machine

Vokabular • vocabulary

drucken
print (v)

vergrößern
enlarge (v)

kopieren
copy (v)

verkleinern
reduce (v)

Ich möchte fotokopieren.
I need to make some copies.

der Bürobedarf • office supplies

der Empfehlungszettel
notecard

der Geschäftsbogen
stationery

der Briefumschlag
envelope

der Aktenordner
box file

der
Kartenreiter
tab

der Teiler
divider

das Klemmbrett
clipboard

der Notizblock
note pad

der Hängeordner
hanging file

der Fächerordner
expanding file

der Leitz-
Ordner
ring binder

die Klammern
staples

der Tesafilm
tape

das Stempelkissen
ink pad

der Terminkalender
personal organizer

der Hefter
stapler

der
Tesafilmhalter
tape dispenser

der Locher
hole punch

der Stempel
rubber stamp

das Gummiband
rubber band

die Papierklammer
bulldog clip

die Büroklammer
paper clip

der
Reißnagel
thumbtack

die Pinnward | notice board

das Büro 2 • office 2

das Flipchart
flipchart

das Protokoll
minutes

das Gestell
easel

der Bericht
report

der Manager
manager

das Angebot
proposal

der leitende Angestellte
executive

die Sitzung | meeting

Vokabular • vocabulary

der Sitzungsraum
meeting room

teilnehmen
attend (v)

die Tagesordnung
agenda

den Vorsitz führen
chair (v)

Um wieviel Uhr ist die Sitzung?
What time is the meeting?

Was sind Ihre Geschäftszeiten?
What are your office hours?

der Projektor
projector

der Sprecher
speaker

die Präsentation | presentation

das Geschäft • business

der Laptop
laptop

die Notizen
notes

der Geschäftsmann
businessman

die Geschäftsfrau
businesswoman

das Arbeitsessen
business lunch

die Geschäftsreise
business trip

der Kunde
client

der Termin
appointment

der Palmtop
palmtop

der
Generaldirektor
CEO

der Terminkalender | organizer

das Geschäftsabkommen
business deal

Vokabular • vocabulary

die Firma company	**das Personal** staff	**die Buchhaltung** accounts department	**die Rechtsabteilung** legal department
die Zentrale headquarters	**die Lohnliste** payroll	**die Marketingabteilung** marketing department	**die Kundendienstabteilung** customer service department
die Zweigstelle regional office	**das Gehalt** salary	**die Verkaufsabteilung** sales department	**die Personalabteilung** human resources department

der Computer • computer

der Drucker
printer

der Monitor
monitor

der Bildschirm
screen

die Zentraleinheit
CPU

der Scanner
scanner

der Lautsprecher
speaker

die Taste
key

die Tastatur
keyboard

die Maus
mouse

die Hardware
hardware

die Diskette
disk

der Laptop
laptop

Vokabular • vocabulary

das RAM RAM	**die Software** software	**der Server** server
die Bytes bytes	**das Programm** program	**der Port** port
das System system	**das Netzwerk** network	**der Prozessor** processor
der Speicher memory	**die Anwendung** application	**das Stromkabel** power cord

das Festplattenlaufwerk
hard drive

das Modem
modem

das Desktop • desktop

der Menübalken
menu bar

die
Werkzeugleiste
toolbar

die Tapete
wallpaper

die Schriftart
font

das Symbol
icon

der Scrollbalken
scrollbar

das Fenster
window

die Datei
file

der Ordner
folder

der Papierkorb
trash

das Internet • internet

die E-Mail • email

der Browser
browser

die Inbox
inbox

die Web-Site
website

browsen
browse (v)

die E-Mail-Adresse
email address

Vokabular • vocabulary

verbinden connect (v)	**der Serviceprovider** service provider	**einloggen** log on (v)	**herunterladen** download (v)	**senden** send (v)	**sichern** save (v)
installieren install (v)	**das E-Mail-Konto** email account	**online** on-line	**der Anhang** attachment	**erhalten** receive (v)	**suchen** search (v)

die Medien • media

das Fernsehstudio • television studio

der Moderator
presenter

die Beleuchtung
light

die Studioeinrichtung
set

die Kamera
camera

der Kamerakran
camera crane

der Kameramann
cameraman

Vokabular • vocabulary

der Kanal channel	**die Nachrichten** news	**die Presse** press	**senden** broadcast (v)	**live** live	**der Zeichentrickfilm** cartoon
die Programm–gestaltung programming	**der Dokumentarfilm** documentary	**die Fernsehserie** television series	**die Spielshow** game show	**vorher aufgezeichnet** prerecorded	**die Seifenoper** soap opera

---

der Interviewer
interviewer

die Reporterin
reporter

der Teleprompter
teleprompter

die Nachrichtensprecherin
newscaster

die Schauspieler
actors

der Mikrophongalgen
sound boom

die Klappe
clapper board

das Set
movie set

das Radio • radio

das **Mischpult**
mixing desk

das **Mikrophon**
microphone

der **Tonmeister**
sound technician

das Tonstudio | recording studio

Vokabular • vocabulary

der DJ DJ	**die Kurzwelle** short wave
die Sendung broadcast	**die Mittelwelle** medium wave
die Wellenlänge wavelength	**die Frequenz** frequency
die Langwelle long wave	**die Lautstärke** volume
die Rundfunkstation radio station	**einstellen** tune (v)

das Recht • law

der Gerichtsdiener
bailiff

der Zeuge
witness

der Richter
judge

der Rechtsanwalt
lawyer

die Geschworenen
jury

die Geschworenen bank
jury box

der Gerichtssaal | courtroom

die Staatsanwaltschaft
prosecution

der Protokollführer
court clerk

Vokabular • vocabulary

das Anwaltsbüro lawyer's office	**die Vorladung** summons	**die Verfügung** writ	**der Rechtsfall** court case
die Rechtsberatung legal advice	**die Aussage** statement	**der Gerichtstermin** court date	**die Anklage** charge
der Klient client	**der Haftbefehl** warrant	**das Plädoyer** plea	**der Angeklagte** accused

der
Gerichtsstenograf
stenographer

der
Straftäter
criminal

der Verdächtige
suspect

der Angeklagte
defendant

die Verteidigung
defense

das Phantombild
composite

das Strafregister
criminal record

der Gefängniswärter
prison guard

die Gefängniszelle
cell

das Gefängnis
prison

Vokabular • vocabulary

das Beweismittel evidence	**schuldig** guilty	**die Kaution** bail	**Ich möchte mit einem Anwalt sprechen.** I want to see a lawyer.
das Urteil verdict	**freigesprochen** acquitted	**die Berufung** appeal	**Wo ist das Gericht?** Where is the courthouse?
unschuldig innocent	**das Strafmaß** sentence	**die Haftentlassung auf Bewährung** parole	**Kann ich die Kaution leisten?** Can I post bail?

---

der Bauernhof 1 • farm 1

das Ackerland
farmland

der Hof
farmyard

das Nebengebäude
outbuilding

das Bauernhaus
farmhouse

der Bauer
farmer

das Feld
field

die Scheune
barn

der Gemüse-garten
vegetable garden

die Hecke
hedge

das Tor
gate

der Zaun
fence

die Weide
pasture

das Vieh
livestock

der Kultivator
cultivator

der Traktor | tractor

der Mähdrescher | combine

die landwirtschaftlichen Betriebe • types of farm

die Feldfrucht
crop

der Ackerbaubetrieb
crop farm

der Betrieb für Milchproduktion
dairy farm

die Herde
flock

die Schaffarm
sheep farm

die Hühnerfarm
poultry farm

die Schweinefarm
pig farm

die Fischzucht
fish farm

der Obstanbau
fruit farm

der Weinstock
vine

der Weinberg
vineyard

die Tätigkeiten • actions

die Furche
furrow

pflügen
plow (v)

säen
sow (v)

melken
milk (v)

füttern
feed (v)

bewässern | water (v)

ernten | harvest (v)

Vokabular • vocabulary

das Herbizid herbicide	**die Herde** herd	**der Trog** trough
das Pestizid pesticide	**der Silo** silo	**pflanzen** plant (v)

der Bauernhof 2 • farm 2

die Feldfrüchte • crops

der Weizen
wheat

der Mais
corn

die Gerste
barley

der Raps
rapeseed

die Sonnenblume
sunflower

der Ballen
bale

das Heu
hay

die Luzerne
alfalfa

der Tabak
tobacco

der Reis
rice

der Tee
tea

der Kaffee
coffee

die Vogelscheuche
scarecrow

der Flachs
flax

das Zuckerrohr
sugarcane

die Baumwolle
cotton

das Vieh • livestock

das Ferkel
piglet

das Kalb
calf

das Schwein
pig

die Kuh
cow

der Stier
bull

das Schaf
sheep

das Zicklein
kid

das Fohlen
foal

das Lamm
lamb

die Ziege
goat

das Pferd
horse

der Esel
donkey

das Küken
chick

das Entenküken
duckling

das Huhn
chicken

der Hahn
rooster

der Truthahn
turkey

die Ente
duck

der Stall
stable

der Pferch
pen

der Hühnerstall
chicken coop

der Schweinestall
pigsty

der Bau • construction

das Gerüst
scaffolding

die Palette
pallet

die Leiter
ladder

das Fenster
window

der
Dachsparren
rafter

der Gabelstapler
forklift truck

die Baustelle
construction site

der Sturz
lintel

die
Mauer
wall

der Werkzeuggürtel
toolbelt

der Balken
beam

der Träger
girder

der
Schutzhelm
hard hat

der Zement
cement

bauen
build (v)

der Bauarbeiter
carpenter

die Betonmischmaschine
cement mixer

das Material • materials

der Ziegelstein
brick

das Bauholz
lumber

der Dachziegel
roof tile

der Betonblock
concrete block

die Werkzeuge • tools

der Mörtel
mortar

die Kelle
trowel

die Wasserwaage
level

der Stiel
handle

der Vorschlaghammer
sledgehammer

die Spitzhacke
pickax

die Schaufel
shovel

die Maschinen • machinery

die Walze
roller

der Kipper
dump truck

die Stütze
support

der Haken
hook

der Kran | crane

die Straßenarbeiten • roadworks

der Asphalt
asphalt

der Leitkegel
cone

der Pressluftbohrer
jackhammer

der Neubelag
resurfacing

der Bagger
excavator

die Berufe 1 • occupations 1

der Schreiner
carpenter

der Elektriker
electrician

der Klempner
plumber

der Bauhandwerker
construction worker

der Gärtner
gardener

der Staubsauger
vacuum cleaner

der Gebäudereiniger
cleaner

der Mechaniker
mechanic

der Metzger
butcher

die Schere
scissors

die Fischhändlerin
fish seller

der Gemüsehändler
produce seller

die Floristin
florist

der Friseur
hairdresser

der Friseur
barber

der Juwelier
jeweler

die Verkäuferin
store clerk

die Maske
mask

die Immobilienmaklerin
realtor

der Optiker
optometrist

die Zahnärztin
dentist

der Arzt
doctor

die Apothekerin
pharmacist

die Krankenschwester
nurse

die Tierärztin
veterinarian

der Bauer
farmer

das Abzeichen
badge

der Fischer
fisherman

**das
Maschinen-
gewehr**
machine-
gun

die Uniform
uniform

der Wächter
security guard

der Seemann
sailor

der Soldat
soldier

der Polizist
police officer

der Feuerwehrmann
firefighter

die Berufe 2 • occupations 2

der Rechtsanwalt
lawyer

der Wirtschaftsprüfer
accountant

das Modell
model

der Architekt
architect

der Wissenschaftler
scientist

die Lehrerin
teacher

der Bibliothekar
librarian

die Empfangsdame
receptionist

die
Posttasche
mailbag

der Briefträger
mail carrier

der Busfahrer
bus driver

der Lastwagenfahrer
truck driver

der Taxifahrer
cab driver

der Pilot
pilot

die Flugbegleiterin
flight attendant

die Reisebürokauffrau
travel agent

die
Kochmütze
chef's hat

der Koch
chef

das
Ballett
röckchen
tutu

der Musiker
musician

die Tänzerin
dancer

der Schauspieler
actor

die Sängerin
singer

die Kellnerin
waitress

der Barkeeper
bartender

der Sportler
sportsman

der Bildhauer
sculptor

die Notizen
notes

die Malerin
painter

der Fotograf
photographer

der Nachrichtensprecher
newscaster

der Journalist
journalist

die Redakteurin
editor

die Designerin
designer

die Damenschneiderin
seamstress

der Schneider
tailor

der Verkehr
transportation

die Straßen • roads

die Autobahn
freeway

die Mautstelle
toll booth

die Straßen-
markierungen
road markings

die
Zufahrtsstraße
frontage road

Einbahn-
one-way

die Verkehrsinsel
divider

die Kreuzung
interchange

die
Verkehrs-
ampel
traffic light

die rechte Spur
right lane

die mittlere Spur
center lane

die Überholspur
left lane

die Ausfahrt
exit ramp

der Verkehr
traffic

die
Überführung
overpass

der Seitenstreifen
shoulder

der
Lastwagen
truck

der Mittelstreifen
median strip

die Unterführung
underpass

die Notrufsäule
emergency phone

der Behindertenparkplatz
disabled parking

der Verkehrsstau
traffic jam

der Fußgängerüberweg
crosswalk

die Landkarte
map

die Parkuhr
parking meter

der Verkehrspolizist
traffic policeman

Vokabular • vocabulary

parken
park (v)

überholen
pass (v)

rückwärts fahren
back up (v)

fahren
drive (v)

abschleppen
tow away (v)

die Umleitung
detour

die Leitplanke
guardrail

die Straßenbaustelle
road construction

die Schnellstraße
divided highway

der Kreisverkehr
roundabout

Ist dies die Straße nach...?
Is this the road to...?

Wo kann ich parken?
Where can I park?

die Verkehrsschilder • road signs

keine Einfahrt
do not enter

die Geschwindigkeitsbegrenzung
speed limit

Gefahr
hazard

Halten verboten
no stopping

rechts abbiegen verboten
no right turn

der Bus • bus

der **Fahrersitz**
driver's seat

der **Haltegriff**
handrail

die **Automatiktür**
automatic door

das **Vorderrad**
front wheel

das **Gepäckfach**
luggage hold

die Tür | door

der Reisebus | long-distance bus

die Bustypen • types of buses

die **Liniennummer**
route number

der **Fahrer**
driver

der Doppeldecker
double-decker bus

die Straßenbahn
tram

der Obus
trolley bus

der Schulbus | school bus

das Hinterrad
rear wheel

das Fenster
window

der Halteknopf
stop button

der Fahrschein
bus ticket

die Klingel
bell

der Busbahnhof
bus station

die
Bushaltestelle
bus stop

Vokabular • vocabulary

der Fahrpreis
fare

der Rollstuhlzugang
wheelchair access

der Fahrplan
schedule

das Wartehäuschen
bus shelter

Halten Sie am…?
Do you stop at…?

Welcher Bus fährt nach…?
Which bus goes to…?

der Kleinbus
minibus

der Touristenbus | tour bus

der Zubringer | shuttle bus

das Auto 1 • car 1

das Äußere • exterior

der Rückspiegel
rear-view mirror

der Scheibenwischer
windshield wiper

die Autotür
door

der Seitenspiegel
side mirror

die Windschutz scheibe
windshield

der Kofferraum
trunk

die Motorhaube
hood

der Blinker
turn signal

die Stoßstange
bumper

das Nummernschild
license plate

der Scheinwerfer
headlight

das Rad
wheel

der Reifen
tire

das Gepäck
luggage

der Dachgepäckträger
roof rack

die Hecktür
tailgate

der Sicherheitsgurt
seat belt

der Kindersitz
car seat

die Wagentypen • types

der Kleinwagen
compact car

die Fließhecklimousine
hatchback

die Limousine
sedan

der Kombiwagen
station wagon

das Kabriolett
convertible

das Sportkabriolett
sports car

**die Großraum-
limousine**
minivan

der Geländewagen
four-wheel drive

das Vorkriegsmodell
vintage

die verlängerte Limousine
limousine

die Tankstelle • gas station

die Zapfsäule
gas pump

der Benzinpreis
price

der Tankstellenplatz
forecourt

**das
Druckluftgerät**
air supply

Vokabular • vocabulary

das Benzin gasoline	**verbleit** leaded	**die Autowaschanlage** carwash
bleifrei unleaded	**das Öl** oil	**das Frostschutzmittel** antifreeze
die Werkstatt garage	**der Diesel** diesel	**die Scheibenwasch anlage** screenwash

Voll tanken, bitte.
Fill it up, please.

das Auto 2 • car 2

die Innenausstattung • interior

der Rücksitz	die Armstütze	die Kopfstütze	die Türverriegelung	der Türgriff
back seat	armrest	headrest	door lock	handle

Vokabular • vocabulary

zweitürig	**viertürig**	**die Zündung**	**die Bremse**	**das Gaspedal**
two-door	four-door	ignition	brake	accelerator
dreitürig	**mit Handschaltung**	**mit Automatik**	**die Kupplung**	**die Klimaanlage**
hatchback	manual	automatic	clutch	air conditioning

Wie komme ich nach...?
Can you tell me the way to...?

Wo ist hier ein Parkplatz?
Where is the parking lot?

Kann ich hier parken?
Can I park here?

die Armaturen • controls

| **das Lenkrad** steering wheel | **die Hupe** horn | **das Armaturenbrett** dashboard | **die Warnlichter** hazard lights | **das GPS-System** satellite navigation |

die Linkssteuerung | left-hand drive

| **die Temperaturanzeige** temperature gauge | **der Drehzahlmesser** tachometer | | **der Tachometer** speedometer | **die Kraftstoffanzeige** fuel gauge |

die Autostereoanlage car stereo

der Lichtschalter light switch

der Heizungsregler heater controls

der Kilometerzähler odometer

der Airbag air bag

der Schalthebel gearstick

die Rechtssteuerung | right-hand drive

das Auto 3 • car 3

die Mechanik • mechanics

der Scheiben
putzmittelbehälter
screen wash reservoir

der Ölmessstab
dipstick

der Luftfilter
air filter

der
Bremsflüssigkeitsbehälter
brake fluid reservoir

die
Batterie
battery

die
Karosserie
bodywork

der Kühlmittelbehälter
coolant reservoir

der
Zylinderkopf
cylinder head

das Rohr
pipe

das
Schiebedach
sunroof

der Kühler
radiator

der Motor
engine

der Ventilator
fan

die
Radkappe
hubcap

das
Getriebe
gearbox

die
Transmission
transmission

die
Kardanwelle
driveshaft

die Reifenpanne • flat tire

das Ersatzrad
spare tire

der Radschlüssel
tire iron

die Radmuttern
wheel nuts

der
Wagenheber
jack

ein Rad wechseln
change a tire (v)

das Dach
roof

die Aufhängung
suspension

der Auspufftopf
muffler

der Auspuff
exhaust pipe

Vokabular • vocabulary

der Autounfall car accident	**der Nockenriemen** cam belt
die Panne breakdown	**der Turbolader** turbocharger
die Versicherung insurance	**der Verteiler** distributor
der Abschleppwagen tow truck	**die Einstellung** timing
der Mechaniker mechanic	**das Chassis** chassis
der Reifendruck tire pressure	**die Handbremse** parking brake
der Sicherungskasten fuse box	**die Lichtmaschine** alternator
die Zündkerze spark plug	**Ich habe eine Panne.** My car has broken down.
der Keilriemen fan belt	**Mein Auto springt nicht an.** My car won't start.
der Benzintank gas tank	

das Motorrad • motorcycle

der
Motorradhelm
helmet

der
Blinker
turn signal

der
Tachometer
speedometer

die **Bremse**
brake

die Kupplung
clutch

die **Hupe**
horn

der **Gashebel**
throttle

die Steuerung
controls

der Gepäckträger
carrier

das Katzenauge
reflector

der **Soziussitz**
pillion

der **Sitz**
seat

der **Motor**
engine

der
Kraftstofftank
fuel tank

das Bremslicht
taillight

das Auspuffrohr
exhaust pipe

der Auspufftopf
muffler

der **Ölsumpf**
oil tank

das Getriebe
gearbox

der Luftfilter
air filter

das Visier
visor

der Lederanzug
leathers

der
Leuchtstreifen
reflector strap

der
Knieschützer
knee pad

die Kleidung | clothing

der Scheinwerfer
headlight

die
Aufhängung
suspension

das
Schutzblech
mudguard

das Bremspedal
brake pedal

die Achse
axle

der Reifen
tire

die Typen • types

die Rennmaschine | racing bike

die Windschutzscheibe
windshield

der Tourer | tourer

das Geländemotorrad | dirt bike

der Motor
radständer
stand

der Roller | scooter

das Fahrrad • bicycle

der Sattel
saddle

die Sattelstütze
seat post

die Wasserflasche
water bottle

der Rahmen
frame

die Felgenbremse
brake

die Nabe
hub

die Gänge
gears

die Felge
rim

der Reifen
tire

die Fahrradkette
chain

das Pedal
pedal

das Zahnrad
cog

das Tandem
tandem

das Rennrad
racing bike

das Mountainbike
mountain bike

das Tourenfahrrad
touring bike

das Straßenrad
road bike

der Fahrradhelm
helmet

der Fahrradweg | cycle lane

deutsch • english

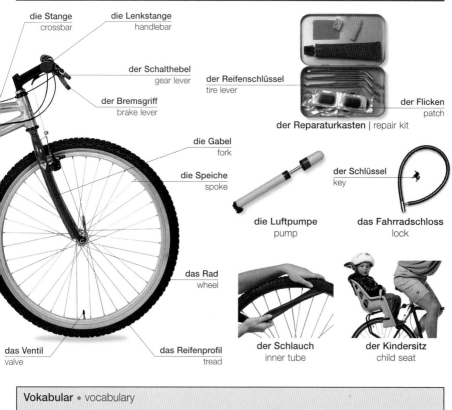

die Stange
crossbar

die Lenkstange
handlebar

der Schalthebel
gear lever

der Reifenschlüssel
tire lever

der Bremsgriff
brake lever

der Flicken
patch

der Reparaturkasten | repair kit

die Gabel
fork

die Speiche
spoke

der Schlüssel
key

die Luftpumpe
pump

das Fahrradschloss
lock

das Rad
wheel

das Ventil
valve

das Reifenprofil
tread

der Schlauch
inner tube

der Kindersitz
child seat

Vokabular • vocabulary

das Rücklicht	die Stützräder	das Kabel	der Korb	der Riemen	bremsen
rear light	training wheels	cable	basket	toe strap	brake (v)
die Fahrradlampe	der Fahrradständer	die Bremsbacke	die Reifenpanne	der Rennbügel	schalten
headlight	kickstand	brake block	flat tire	toe clip	change gears (v)
der Rückstrahler	der Fahrradständer	das Kettenzahnrad	der Dynamo	treten	Rad fahren
reflector	bike rack	sprocket	dynamo	pedal (v)	cycle (v)

---

der Zug • train

der
Wagen
car

die
Gleisnummer
platform number

der
Bahnsteig
platform

der Pendler
commuter

der
Kofferkuli
cart

der Bahnhof | train station

die Zugtypen • types of train

die
Lokomotive
engine

der Führerstand
engineer's cab

die Schiene
rail

die Dampflokomotive
steam train

die Diesellokomotive | diesel train

die Elektrolokomotive
electric train

der Hochgeschwindigkeitszug
high-speed train

die Einschienenbahn
monorail

die U-Bahn
subway

die Straßenbahn
tram

der Güterzug
freight train

die Gepäckablage
luggage rack

das Zugfenster
window

das Gleis
track

die Tür   der Sitz
door   seat

die Eingangssperre
ticket gate

das Abteil
compartment

der Lautsprecher
public address system

der
Fahrplan
schedule

die Fahrkarte
ticket

der Speisewagen | dining car

die Bahnhofshalle | concourse

das Schlafabteil
sleeping compartment

Vokabular • vocabulary

das Bahnnetz rail network	**der U-Bahnplan** subway map	**der Fahrkartenschalter** ticket office	**die stromführende Schiene** live rail
der Intercity express train	**die Verspätung** delay	**der Schaffner** ticket inspector	**das Signal** signal
die Stoßzeit rush hour	**der Fahrpreis** fare	**umsteigen** change (v)	**der Nothebel** emergency lever

das Flugzeug • aircraft

das Verkehrsflugzeug • airliner

der Bug
nose

das Cockpit
cockpit

das Triebwerk
engine

der Rumpf
fuselage

die Tragfläche
wing

das Heck
tail

das Seitenruder
rudder

der Ausgang
exit

das Bugfahrwerk
nosewheel

das Hauptfahrwerk
landing gear

das Querruder
aileron

das Seiten leitwerk
fin

das Höhen leitwerk
tailplane

die Kabine • cabin

der Notausgang
emergency exit

die Flugbegleiterin
flight attendant

das Gepäckfach
overhead bin

die Luftdüse
air vent

das Fenster
window

die Leselampe
reading light

der Sitz
seat

die Reihe
row

die Armlehne
armrest

der Gang
aisle

der Klapptisch
tray-table

die Rückenlehne
seat back

das Ultraleichtflugzeug
ultralight

das Segelflugzeug
glider

der Doppeldecker
biplane

der Propeller
propeller

der Heißluftballon
hot-air balloon

das Leichtflugzeug
light aircraft

das Wasserflugzeug
sea plane

der Privatjet
private jet

das Überschallflugzeug
supersonic jet

das Rotorblatt
rotor blade

die Rakete
missile

der Hubschrauber
helicopter

das Bombenflugzeug
bomber

das Jagdflugzeug
fighter plane

Vokabular • vocabulary

der Pilot pilot	**starten** take off (v)	**landen** land (v)	**die Economyclass** economy class	**das Handgepäck** carry-on luggage
der Kopilot copilot	**fliegen** fly (v)	**die Höhe** altitude	**die Businessclass** business class	**der Sicherheitsgurt** seat belt

---

der Flughafen • airport

das Vorfeld
apron

der
Gepäckanhänger
baggage trailer

der Terminal
terminal

das Versorgungsfahrzeug
service vehicle

die Fluggastbrücke
walkway

das Verkehrsflugzeug | airliner

Vokabular • vocabulary

das Gepäckband carousel	**die Flugnummer** flight number	**die Start- und Landebahn** runway	**der Urlaub** vacation
der Auslandsflug international flight	**die Passkontrolle** immigration	**die Sicherheitsvorkehrungen** security	**einen Flug buchen** book a flight (v)
der Inlandsflug domestic flight	**der Zoll** customs	**die Gepäckröntgenmaschine** X-ray machine	**einchecken** check in (v)
die Flugverbindung connection	**das Übergepäck** excess baggage	**der Urlaubsprospekt** travel brochure	**der Kontrollturm** control tower

das Handgepäck
carry-on luggage

das Gepäck
luggage

der Kofferkuli
cart

der Abfertigungsschalter
check-in desk

der Pass | passport

das Visum
visa

die Passkontrolle
passport control

die Bordkarte
boarding pass

das Flugticket
ticket

die Abflughalle
departure lounge

die Gatenummer
gate number

der Abflug
departures

das Reiseziel
destination

die Ankunft
arrivals

die Fluginformationsanzeige
information screen

der Duty-free-Shop
duty-free shop

die Gepäckausgabe
baggage claim

der Taxistand
taxi stand

der Autoverleih
car rental

das Schiff • ship

die Funkantenne
radio antenna

der Schornstein
funnel

der Radar
radar

der Bug
prow

das Deck
deck

das Achterdeck
quarterdeck

die Höchsttlademarke
load line

das Bullauge
porthole

der Rumpf
hull

das Rettungsboot
lifeboat

der Kiel
keel

die Schiffsschraube
propeller

der Ozeandampfer
ocean liner

die Kommandobrücke
bridge

der Maschinenraum
engine room

die Kabine
cabin

die Kombüse
galley

Vokabular • vocabulary

das Dock dock	**die Ankerwinde** windlass
der Hafen port	**der Kapitän** captain
die Landungsbrücke gangway	**das Rennboot** speedboat
der Anker anchor	**das Ruderboot** rowboat
der Poller bollard	**das Kanu** canoe

andere Schiffe • other ships

die Fähre
ferry

der
Außenbordmotor
outboard motor

das Schlauchboot
inflatable dinghy

das Tragflügelboot
hydrofoil

die Jacht
yacht

der Katamaran
catamaran

der Schleppdampfer
tugboat

das Luftkissenboot
hovercraft

das Containerschiff
container ship

die Takelung
rigging

das Segelboot
sailboat

der
Frachtraum
hold

das Frachtschiff
freighter

der Öltanker
oil tanker

der Flugzeugträger
aircraft carrier

das Kriegsschiff
battleship

der
Kommandoturm
conning tower

das U-Boot
submarine

der Hafen • port

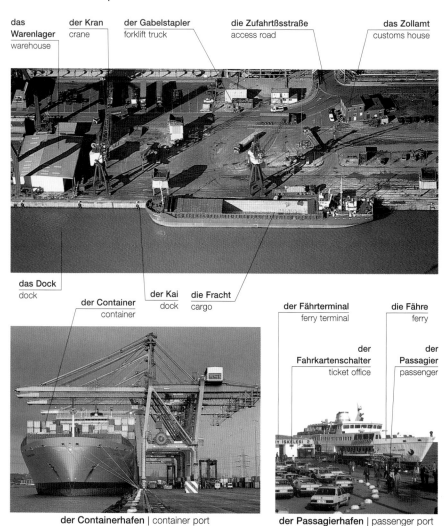

das **Warenlager** warehouse

der **Kran** crane

der **Gabelstapler** forklift truck

die **Zufahrtßsstraße** access road

das **Zollamt** customs house

das **Dock** dock

der **Container** container

der **Kai** dock

die **Fracht** cargo

der **Fährterminal** ferry terminal

die **Fähre** ferry

der **Fahrkartenschalter** ticket office

der **Passagier** passenger

der Containerhafen | container port

der Passagierhafen | passenger port

das Netz
net

das Fischerboot
fishing boat

die Verankerung
mooring

die Marina
marina

der Fischereihafen
fishing port

der Hafen
harbor

der Pier
pier

der Landungssteg
jetty

die Werft
shipyard

die Laterne
lamp

der Leuchtturm
lighthouse

die Boje
buoy

Vokabular • vocabulary

die Küstenwache coastguard	**festmachen** moor (v)	**an Bord gehen** board (v)
der Hafenmeister harbor master	**anlegen** dock (v)	**von Bord gehen** disembark (v)
das Trockendock dry dock	**den Anker werfen** drop anchor (v)	**auslaufen** set sail (v)

der Sport
sports

der Football • football

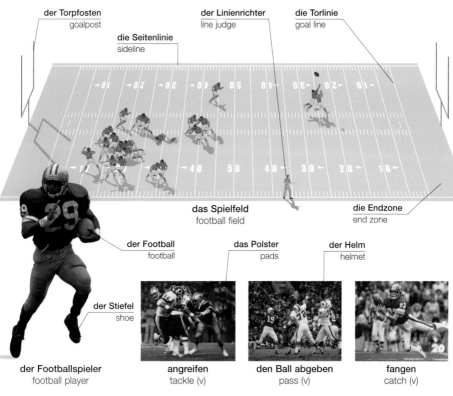

der Torpfosten
goalpost

der Linienrichter
line judge

die Torlinie
goal line

die Seitenlinie
sideline

das Spielfeld
football field

die Endzone
end zone

der Football
football

das Polster
pads

der Helm
helmet

der Stiefel
shoe

der Footballspieler
football player

angreifen
tackle (v)

den Ball abgeben
pass (v)

fangen
catch (v)

Vokabular • vocabulary

die Auszeit time out	**die Mannschaft** team	**die Verteidigung** defense	**der Cheerleader** cheerleader	**Wie ist der Stand?** What is the score?
das unsichere Fangen des Balls fumble	**der Angriff** attack	**der Spielstand** score	**der Touchdown** touchdown	**Wer gewinnt?** Who is winning?

das Rugby • rugby

das Tor
goal

der Torraum
in-goal area

die Seitenlinie
touch line

die Fahne
flag

die Feldauslinie
dead ball line

das Spielfeld | rugby field

der Rugbyball
ball

das
Rugbytrikot
rugby
uniform

werfen
throw (v)

kicken
kick (v)

den Ball abgeben
pass (v)

angreifen
tackle (v)

der Versuch
try

der Rugbyspieler
player

das offene Gedränge | ruck

das Gedränge | scrum

der Fußball • soccer

der Fußball
football

der
Mittelstürmer
forward

der Schiedsrichter
referee

der Mittelkreis
center circle

der Torwart
goalkeeper

der Dress
soccer
uniform

der Fußballspieler
soccer player

das Fußballfeld
soccer field

der Torpfosten
goalpost

die Querlatte
crossbar

das Tornetz
net

dribbeln | dribble (v)

köpfen
head (v)

die Mauer
wall

das Tor | goal

der Freistoß | free kick

der Strafraum
penalty area

die Torlinie
goal line

der Torraum
goal area

das Tor
goal

der Verteidiger
defender

der Linienrichter
linesman

die Eckfahne
corner flag

der Einwurf
throw-in

kicken
kick (v)

der Fußballschuh
shoe

den Ball abgeben
pass (v)

schießen
shoot (v)

halten
save (v)

angreifen
tackle (v)

Vokabular • vocabulary

das Stadion stadium	**das Foul** foul	**die gelbe Karte** yellow card	**die Liga** league	**die Verlängerung** extra time
der Elfmeter penalty	**der Eckball** corner	**das Abseits** off-side	**die Halbzeit** half time	**der Ersatzspieler** substitute
ein Tor schießen score a goal (v)	**die rote Karte** red card	**der Platzverweis** send off	**das Unentschieden** tie	**die Auswechslung** substitution

---

das Hockey • hockey

das Eishockey • ice hockey

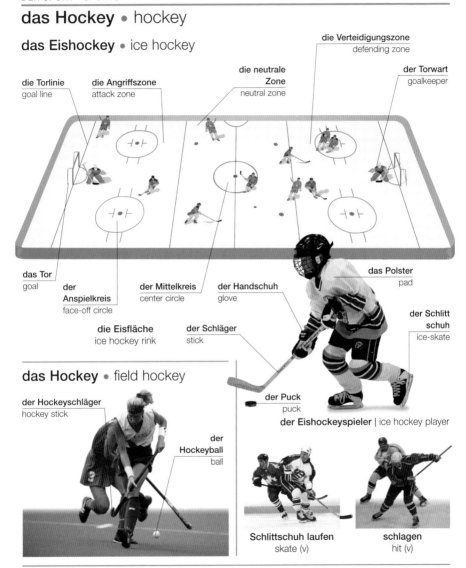

die Verteidigungszone
defending zone

die neutrale Zone
neutral zone

der Torwart
goalkeeper

die Torlinie
goal line

die Angriffszone
attack zone

das Tor
goal

der Anspielkreis
face-off circle

der Mittelkreis
center circle

der Handschuh
glove

das Polster
pad

der Schlitt schuh
ice-skate

die Eisfläche
ice hockey rink

der Schläger
stick

das Hockey • field hockey

der Hockeyschläger
hockey stick

der Hockeyball
ball

der Puck
puck

der Eishockeyspieler | ice hockey player

Schlittschuh laufen
skate (v)

schlagen
hit (v)

das Kricket • cricket

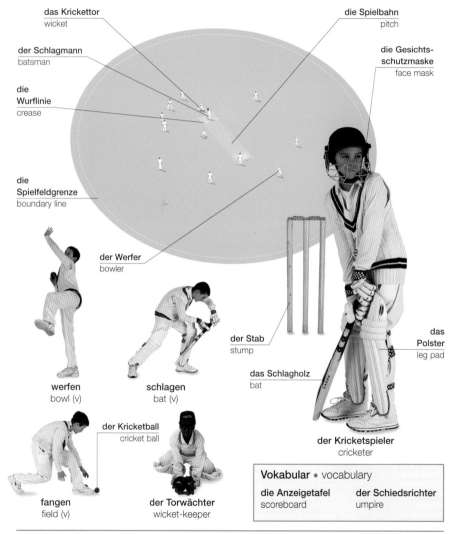

das Krickettor
wicket

die Spielbahn
pitch

der Schlagmann
batsman

die Gesichts-
schutzmaske
face mask

die
Wurflinie
crease

die
Spielfeldgrenze
boundary line

der Werfer
bowler

der Stab
stump

das
Polster
leg pad

das Schlagholz
bat

werfen
bowl (v)

schlagen
bat (v)

der Kricketball
cricket ball

der Kricketspieler
cricketer

fangen
field (v)

der Torwächter
wicket-keeper

Vokabular • vocabulary	
die Anzeigetafel	**der Schiedsrichter**
scoreboard	umpire

der Basketball • basketball

die **Seitenlinie**
sideline

der **Schiedsrichter**
referee

der **Mittelkreis**
center circle

die **Freiwurflinie**
free-throw line

die **Endlinie**
endline

das **Spielfeld**
court

die **Mittellinie**
centerline

die **Dreipunktlinie**
three-point line

das **Korbbrett**
backboard

die **Spieler nummer**
number

der **Basket-ball**
ball

der **Korbring**
hoop

das **Netz**
net

der **Korb**
basket

der Basketballspieler | basketball player

Vokabular • vocabulary

der **Pass** pass	der **Einwurf** throw-in
das **Foul** foul	**aus** out of bounds
der **Rebound** rebound	der **Schiedsricher-ball** jump ball

die Aktionen • actions

werfen
throw (v)

fangen
catch (v)

schießen
shoot (v)

springen
jump (v)

decken
mark (v)

blocken
block (v)

springen lassen
dribble (v)

einen Dunk spielen
dunk (v)

der Volleyball • volleyball

blocken
block (v)

das Netz
net

baggern
dig (v)

der Schiedsrichter
referee

der Knieschützer
knee support

das Spielfeld | court

der Baseball • baseball

das Spielfeld • field

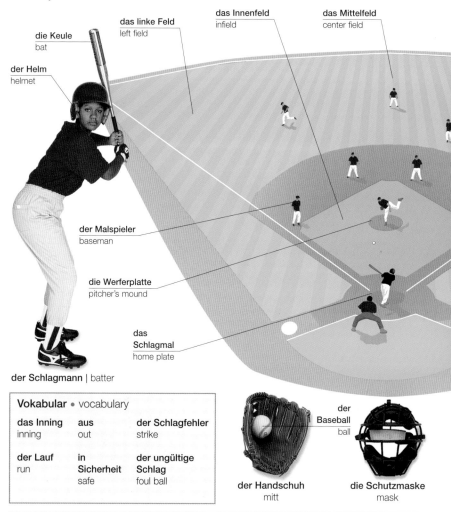

die Keule
bat

der Helm
helmet

das linke Feld
left field

das Innenfeld
infield

das Mittelfeld
center field

der Malspieler
baseman

die Werferplatte
pitcher's mound

das
Schlagmal
home plate

der Schlagmann | batter

der
Baseball
ball

Vokabular • vocabulary

das Inning inning	aus out	der Schlagfehler strike
der Lauf run	in Sicherheit safe	der ungültige Schlag foul ball

der Handschuh
mitt

die Schutzmaske
mask

das Außenfeld
outfield

das rechte Feld
right field

die Foullinie
foul line

die Aktionen • actions

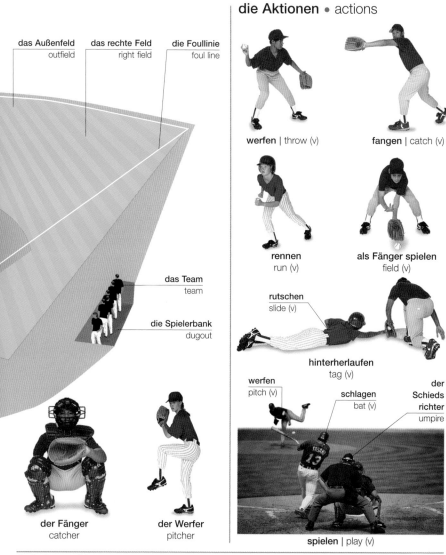

werfen | throw (v)

fangen | catch (v)

rennen
run (v)

als Fänger spielen
field (v)

rutschen
slide (v)

hinterherlaufen
tag (v)

werfen
pitch (v)

schlagen
bat (v)

der
Schieds
richter
umpire

das Team
team

die Spielerbank
dugout

der Fänger
catcher

der Werfer
pitcher

spielen | play (v)

das Tennis • tennis

der Griff
handle

der Kopf
head

die Saite
string

der Schiedsrichter
umpire

die Grundlinie
baseline

der Tennis-
schläger
racket

die Aufschlaglinie
service line

die Seitenlinie
sideline

der Tennisball
ball

das
Schweißband
wristband

der Tennisplatz | tennis court

Vokabular • vocabulary					
das Einzel singles	**der Satz** set	**der Einstand** deuce	**der Fehler** fault	**der Slice** slice	**der Spin** spin
das Doppel doubles	**das Match** match	**der Vorteil** advantage	**das Ass** ace	**Netz!** let!	**der Linienrichter** linesman
das Spiel game	**der Tiebreak** tiebreak	**null** love	**der Stoppball** dropshot	**der Ballwechsel** rally	**die Meisterschaft** championship

die Schläge • strokes

das Netz
net

der Schmetterball
smash

der Balljunge
ball boy

aufschlagen
serve (v)

die Tennisschuhe
tennis shoes

der Tennisspieler
player

der Aufschlag
serve

der Volley
volley

der Return
return

der Lob
lob

die Vorhand
forehand

die Rückhand
backhand

die Schlägerspiele • racket games

der Federball
shuttlecock

der Tischtennisschläger
paddle

das Badminton
badminton

das Tischtennis
table tennis

das Squash
squash

das Racquetball
racquetball

das Golf • golf

das Grün
green

der Bunker
bunker

die Flagge
flag

der Abschlag
teeing ground

das Loch
hole

schwingen
swing (v)

das Fairway
fairway

das Rough
rough

das Wasserhindernis
water hazard

der Golfplatz
golf course

der Buggy
golf cart

die Haltung
stance

der Golfspieler | golfer

das Klubhaus | clubhouse

die Ausrüstung • equipment

die Golf-schläger • golf clubs

der Schirm
umbrella

der Golfball
golf ball

die Golftasche
golf bag

das Tee
tee

die Spikes
spikes

das Holz
wood

der Handschuh
glove

der Caddie
golf cart

der Golfschuh
golf shoe

der Putter
putter

die Aktionen • actions

vom Abschlag
spielen
tee off (v)

driven
drive (v)

einlochen
putt (v)

chippen
chip (v)

das Eisen
iron

das Wedge
wedge

Vokabular • vocabulary

das Par par	über Par over par	das Golfturnier tournament	der Caddie caddy	der Schlag stroke	die Spielbahn line of play
unter Par par	das Hole-in- One hole in one	das Handicap handicap	die Zuschauer spectators	der Übungsschwung practice swing	der Durchschwung backswing

---

die Leichtathletik • track and field

die Bahn
lane

die Rennbahn
track

die Ziellinie
finish line

die Startlinie
starting line

das Feld
field

die Leichtathletin
athlete

der Startblock
starting blocks

der Sprinter
sprinter

das Diskuswerfen
discus

das Kugelstoßen
shotput

das Speerwerfen
javelin

Vokabular • vocabulary

das Rennen race	**der Rekord** record	**das Fotofinish** photo finish	**der Stabhochsprung** pole vault
die Zeit time	**einen Rekord brechen** break a record (v)	**der Marathon** marathon	**die persönliche Bestleistung** personal best

die Stoppuhr
stopwatch

234

der Stab
baton

die Latte
crossbar

der Staffellauf
relay race

der Hochsprung
high jump

der Weitsprung
long jump

der Hürdenlauf
hurdles

das Turnen • gymnastics

das Sprungbrett
springboard

die Turnerin
gymnast

das Pferd
horse

der Salto
somersault

der Schwebebalken
beam

das Gymnastikband
ribbon

die Matte
mat

der Sprung
vault

das Bodenturnen
floor exercises

die Bodenakrobatik
tumble

die rhythmische Gymnastik
rhythmic gymnastics

Vokabular • vocabulary

das Reck horizontal bar	**der Stufenbarren** asymmetric bars	**die Ringe** rings	**die Medaillen** medals	**das Silber** silver
der Barren parallel bars	**das Seitpferd** pommel horse	**das Siegerpodium** podium	**das Gold** gold	**die Bronze** bronze

---

der Kampfsport • combat sports

der Gegner
opponent

der Kopfschutz
guard

der Handschuh
glove

der Gürtel
belt

das Taekwondo
tae kwon do

das Karate
karate

das Judo
judo

die Maske
mask

der Säbel
sword

das Kung-Fu
kung fu

das Aikido
aikido

das Kendo
kendo

das Kickboxen
kickboxing

das Ringen
wrestling

das Boxen
boxing

die Techniken • actions

das Fallen fall	**der Griff** hold	**der Wurf** throw	**das Fesseln** pin
der Seitfußstoß kick	**der Stoß** punch	**der Angriff** strike	
der Sprung jump	**der Block** block	**der Hieb** chop	

Vokabular • vocabulary

der Boxring boxing ring	**die Runde** round	**die Faust** fist	**der schwarze Gürtel** black belt	**das Capoeira** capoeira
die Boxhandschuhe boxing gloves	**der Kampf** bout	**der Knockout** knockout	**die Selbstverteidigung** self-defense	**das Sumo** sumo wrestling
der Mundschutz mouth guard	**das Sparren** sparring	**der Sandsack** punching bag	**die Kampfsportarten** martial arts	**das Tai Chi** tai chi

der Schwimmsport • swimming
die Ausrüstung • equipment

der Schwimmflügel
armband

die Schwimmbrille
goggles

die Nasenklemme
nose clip

das Schwimmfloß
kickboard

der Badeanzug
swimsuit

die Badekappe
cap

die Bahn
lane

das Wasser
water

der Startblock
starting block

die Badehose
trunks

das Schwimmbecken
swimming pool

der Schwimmer | swimmer

das Sprungbrett
springboard

der Springer
diver

springen | dive (v)

schwimmen | swim (v)

die Kehre | turn

die Schwimmstile • styles

das Kraulen
front crawl

das Brustschwimmen
breaststroke

der Zug
stroke

der Stoß
kick

das Rückenschwimmen | backstroke

der Butterfly | butterfly

das Tauchen • scuba diving

die Druckluftflasche
air cylinder

der Taucheranzug
wetsuit

der Schnorchel
snorkel

die Tauchermaske
mask

die Schwimmflosse
flipper

der Bleigürtel
weight belt

der Lungenautomat
regulator

Vokabular • vocabulary

der Sprung dive	**Wasser treten** tread water (v)	**das tiefe Ende** deep end	**der Wasserball** water polo	**das flache Ende** shallow end	**der Krampf** cramp
der Turmsprung high dive	**der Startsprung** racing dive	**die Schließfächer** lockers	**der Bademeister** lifeguard	**das Synchronschwimmen** synchronized swimming	**ertrinken** drown (v)

der Segelsport • sailing

der Kompass
compass

der Anker
anchor

der Mast
mast

die Takelung
rigging

das Großsegel
mainsail

der Baum
boom

das Heck
stern

die Klampe
cleat

die Fock
headsail

das Seitendeck
sidedeck

der Bug
bow

die Pinne
tiller

der Rumpf
hull

navigieren | navigate (v)

die Segeljacht | yacht

die Sicherheit • safety

die Leuchtrakete
flare

der Rettungsring
life preserver

die Schwimmweste
life jacket

das Rettungsboot
life raft

der Wassersport • watersports

der Ruderer
rower

das Ruder
oar

das Kajak
kayak

das Paddel
paddle

rudern | row (v)

der Kanusport
canoeing

das Segel
sail

das Surfbrett
surfboard

der Wasserski
ski

der Windsurfer
windsurfer

das Wellenreiten
surfing

das Wasserski
waterskiing

der Schnellbootsport
speed-boating

**das
Surfbrett**
board

die Fußschlaufe
footstrap

das Rafting
rafting

der Wassermotorradsport
jet skiing

das Windsurfing | windsurfing

Vokabular • vocabulary

der Surfer surfer	**die Crew** crew	**der Wind** wind	**die Brandung** surf	**die Schot** sheet	**das Schwert** centerboard
der Wasserskifahrer waterskier	**aufkreuzen** tack (v)	**die Welle** wave	**das Wildwasser** rapids	**das Ruder** rudder	**kentern** capsize (v)

der Reitsport • horse riding

der Reithelm
riding hat

die Mähne
mane

der Reiter
rider

der Sattel
saddle

die Zügel
reins

das Pferd
horse

die Reithose
jodhpurs

der Schweif
tail

der Sattelgurt
girth

der Reitstiefel
riding boot

der Steigbügel
stirrup

der Vorderzwiesel
pommel

der Huf
hoof

der Nasenriemen
noseband

der Stirnriemen
browband

die Kandare
bit

der Sitz
seat

das Hufeisen
horseshoe

der Damensattel
side-saddle

das Zaumzeug | bridle

die Reitgerte | riding crop

die Veranstaltungen • events

das Rennpferd
racehorse

das Hindernis
fence

das Pferderennen
horse race

das Jagdrennen
steeplechase

das Trabrennen
harness race

das Rodeo
rodeo

das Springreiten
showjumping

das Zweispännerrennen
carriage race

das Trekking
trail riding

das Dressurreiten
dressage

das Polo
polo

Vokabular • vocabulary

der Schritt walk	**der Kanter** canter	**der Sprung** jump	**das Halfter** halter	**die Koppel** paddock	**das Flachrennen** flat race
der Trab trot	**der Galopp** gallop	**der Stallbursche** groom	**der Pferdestall** stable	**der Turnierplatz** arena	**die Rennbahn** racecourse

der Angelsport • fishing

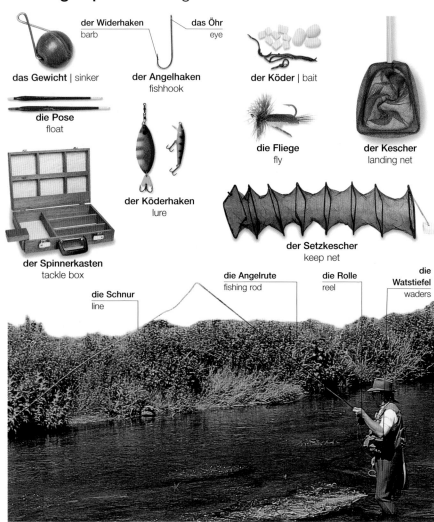

der Widerhaken
barb

das Öhr
eye

das Gewicht | sinker

der Angelhaken
fishhook

der Köder | bait

die Pose
float

die Fliege
fly

der Kescher
landing net

der Köderhaken
lure

der Setzkescher
keep net

der Spinnerkasten
tackle box

die Angelrute
fishing rod

die Rolle
reel

die Watstiefel
waders

die Schnur
line

der Angler | angler

die Fischfangarten • types of fishing

das Süßwasserangeln
freshwater fishing

das Fliegenangeln
fly fishing

das Sportangeln
sport fishing

die Hochseefischerei
deep sea fishing

das Brandungsangeln
surfcasting

die Aktivitäten • activities

auswerfen
cast (v)

fangen
catch (v)

einholen
reel in (v)

mit dem Netz fangen
net (v)

loslassen
release (v)

Vokabular • vocabulary

ködern bait (v)	**die Angelgeräte** tackle	**die Regenhaut** waterproofs	**der Angelschein** fishing permit	**der Fischkorb** creel
anbeißen bite (v)	**die Rolle** spool	**die Stake** pole	**die Seefischerei** marine fishing	**das Speerfischen** spearfishing

---

der Skisport • skiing

der Skihang
ski slope

der Sessellift
chairlift

der Kabinenlift
cable car

der Skianzug
ski suit

der Skistock
ski pole

der Handschuh
glove

die Skipiste
ski run

die Sicherheitssperre
safety barrier

der Skistiefel
ski boot

der Ski
ski

die Kante
edge

die Skiläuferin
skier

die Spitze
tip

die Disziplinen • events

der Abfahrtslauf
downhill skiing

das Tor
gate

der Slalom
slalom

der Skisprung
ski jump

der Langlauf
cross-country skiing

der Wintersport • winter sports

das Eisklettern
ice climbing

das Eislaufen
ice-skating

die Skibrille
goggles

der Schlittschuh
skate

der Eiskunstlauf
figure skating

das Snowboarding
snowboarding

der Bobsport
bobsled

das Rennrodeln
luge

das Schneemobil
snowmobile

das Schlittenfahren
sledding

Vokabular • vocabulary

die alpine Kombination alpine skiing	**das Hundeschlittenfahren** dog-sledding
der Riesenslalom giant slalom	**das Eisschnelllauf** speed skating
abseits der Piste off-piste	**das Biathlon** biathlon
das Curling curling	**die Lawine** avalanche

die anderen Sportarten • other sports

das Segelflugzeug
glider

der Drachen
hang-glider

das Segelfliegen
gliding

der Fallschirm
parachute

das Drachenfliegen
hang-gliding

das Seil
rope

das Klettern
rock-climbing

das Fallschirmspringen
parachuting

das Gleitschirmfliegen
paragliding

das Fallschirmspringen
skydiving

das Abseilen
rappelling

das Bungeejumping
bungee jumping

der
Rennfahrer
racing driver

das Rallyefahren
rally driving

der Rennsport
auto racing

das Motocross
motocross

das Motorradrennen
motorcycle racing

das Skateboard
skateboard

der Lacrosseschläger
stick

das Florett
foil

die Maske
mask

der Rollschuh
rollerskate

**das Skateboard-
fahren**
skateboarding

das Rollschuhfahren
rollerskating

das Lacrosse
lacrosse

das Fechten
fencing

der Kegel
pin

der Bogen
bow

die Zielscheibe
target

der Pfeil
arrow

der Köcher
quiver

das Bogenschießen
archery

**das
Scheibenschießen**
target shooting

**die
Bowlingkugel**
bowling ball

das Bowling
bowling

das Poolbillard
pool

das Snooker
snooker

die Fitness • fitness

das Trainingsrad
exercise bike

das Fitnessgerät
gym machine

die Bank
bench

die Gewichte
free weights

die Stange
bar

das Fitnesscenter
gym

die Rudermaschine
rowing machine

das Laufband
treadmill

die Langlaufmaschine
cross-trainer

die private Fitness-
trainerin
personal trainer

die Tretmaschine
step machine

das Schwimmbecken
swimming pool

die Sauna
sauna

die Übungen • exercises

die Strumpfhose
tights

das Strecken
stretch

der Ausfall
lunge

der Liegestütz
pushup

die Hantel
dumbbell

die Kniebeuge
squat

das Rumpfheben
situp

die Bizepsübung
biceps curl

der Beinstütz
leg press

Trainings
schuhe
athletic
shoes

die Gewicht
hantel
weight bar

das Hemd
vest

die Brustübung
chest press

das Krafttraining
weight training

das Jogging
jogging

das Aerobic
aerobics

Vokabular • vocabulary

trainieren train (v)	**beugen** flex (v)	**ausstrecken** extend (v)	**die Pilates-Übungen** Pilates	**das Zirkeltraining** circuit training
sich **aufwärmen** warm up (v)	**auf der Stelle** **joggen** jog in place (v)	**hochziehen** pull up (v)	**die Boxgymnastik** boxercise	**das Seilspringen** jumping rope

---

die Freizeit
leisure

das Theater • theater

der Vorhang
curtain

die Kulisse
wings

das
Bühnenbild
set

das Publikum
audience

das Orchester
orchestra

die Bühne | stage

der Sitzplatz
seat

der zweite Rang
balcony

die Reihe
row

die Loge
box

der erste
Rang
balcony

der
Balkon
balcony

der Gang
aisle

das
Parkett
orchestra

die Bestuhlung | seating

Vokabular • vocabulary

das Theaterstück play	**der Regisseur** director	**die Premiere** first night
die Besetzung cast	**der Prospekt** backdrop	**die Pause** intermission
der Schauspieler actor	**das Rollenheft** script	**das Programm** program
die Schauspielerin actress	**der Regisseur** producer	**der Orchestergraben** orchestra pit

das Konzert
concert

das Musical
musical

das
Theaterkostüm
costume

das Ballett
ballet

Vokabular • vocabulary

der Platzanweiser usher	**die Tonspur** soundtrack	**Ich möchte zwei Karten für die Aufführung heute Abend.** I'd like two tickets for tonight's performance.
die klassische Musik classical music	**applaudieren** applaud (v)	
die Noten musical score	**die Zugabe** encore	**Um wieviel Uhr beginnt die Aufführung?** What time does it start?

die Oper
opera

das Kino • cinema

das
Popcorn
popcorn

die Kasse
box office

das Foyer
lobby

das
Plakat
poster

der Kinosaal
movie theater

die Leinwand
screen

Vokabular • vocabulary

die Komödie comedy	**der Liebesfilm** romance
der Thriller thriller	**der Science-Fiction-Film** science fiction movie
der Horrorfilm horror movie	**der Abenteuerfilm** adventure
der Western western	**der Zeichentrickfilm** animated film

das Orchester • orchestra

die Saiteninstrumente • strings

die Harfe
harp

der Dirigent
conductor

der Kontrabass
double bass

die Geige
violin

das Podium
podium

die Bratsche
viola

das Cello
cello

die Noten
score

der
Violinschlüssel
treble clef

die Note
note

das
Liniensystem
staff

der
Bassschlüssel
bass clef

die Notation | notation

das Klavier | piano

Vokabular • vocabulary

die Ouvertüre overture	die Sonate sonata	die Tonhöhe pitch	das Kreuz sharp	der Taktstrich bar	die Tonleiter scale
die Symphonie symphony	die Musikinstrumente instruments	das Pausenzeichen rest	das B flat	das Auflösungszeichen natural	der Taktstock baton

die Holzblasinstrumente • woodwind

die Pikkoloflöte
piccolo

die Querflöte
flute

die Oboe
oboe

das Englischhorn
cor anglais

die Klarinette
clarinet

die Bassklarinette
bass clarinet

das Fagott
bassoon

das Kontrafagott
double bassoon

das Saxophon
saxophone

die Schlaginstrumente • percussion

die Bongos
bongos

die kleine Trommel
snare drum

die Kesselpauke
kettledrum

der Gong
gong

das Becken
cymbals

das Tamburin
tambourine

das Vibraphon
vibraphone

der Triangel
triangle

die Maracas
maracas

die Blechblasinstrumente • brass

die Trompete
trumpet

die Posaune
trombone

das Horn
French horn

die Tuba
tuba

das Konzert • concert

der
Leadsänger
lead singer

das Mikrophon
microphone

der
Schlag-
zeuger
drummer

der Gitarrist
guitarist

die Fans
fans

der Bassgitarrist
bass guitarist

der
Lautsprecher
speaker

das Rockkonzert | rock concert

die Instrumente • instruments

der
Tonabnehmer
pickup

der Hals
neck

der Bund
fret

der Wirbel
tuning peg

die Saite
string

der Steg
bridge

die
Trommel
drum

die Bassgitarre
bass guitar

das Keyboard
keyboard

die elektrische Gitarre
electric guitar

das Schlagzeug
drum kit

die Musikstile • musical styles

der Jazz
jazz

der Blues
blues

die Punkmusik
punk

der Folk
folk music

der Pop
pop

die Tanzmusik
dance

der Rap
rap

das Heavymetal
heavy metal

die klassische Musik
classical music

Vokabular • vocabulary					
das Lied song	**der Text** lyrics	**die Melodie** melody	**der Beat** beat	**der Reggae** reggae	**die Countrymusic** country

die Besichtigungstour • sightseeing

die Route
itinerary

mit offenem
Oberdeck
open-top

der Tourist
tourist

der Stadtrundfahrtbus | tour bus

die Touristenattraktion | tourist attraction

die
Fremdenführerin
tour guide

die Figur
statuette

die Führung
guided tour

die Andenken
souvenirs

Vokabular • vocabulary

geöffnet open	**der Film** film	**der Camcorder** camcorder	**links** left	**Wo ist…?** Where is…?
geschlossen closed	**die Batterien** batteries	**die Kamera** camera	**rechts** right	**Ich habe mich verlaufen.** I'm lost.
das Eintrittsgeld admission charge	**der Reiseführer** guidebook	**die Richtungs-angaben** directions	**geradeaus** straight ahead	**Können Sie mir sagen, wie ich nach… komme?** Can you tell me the way to….?

---

die Sehenswürdigkeiten • attractions

das
Gemälde
painting

das
**Aussellungs
stück**
exhibit

die
Ausstellung
exhibition

die berühmte
Ruine
famous ruin

die Kunstgalerie
art gallery

das Monument
monument

das Museum
museum

**das historische
Gebäude**
historic building

das Kasino
casino

der Park
gardens

der Nationalpark
national park

die Information • information

die **Zeiten**
times

der Grundriss
floor plan

der Stadtplan
map

der Fahrplan
schedule

**die
Touristeninformation**
tourist information

die Aktivitäten im Freien • outdoor activities

der Fußweg footpath

die Sonnenuhr sundial

das Café café

der Park | park

das Gras grass

die Bank bench

die Gartenanlagen formal gardens

die Berg-und-Talbahn roller coaster

der Jahrmarkt fairground

der Vergnügungspark theme park

der Safaripark safari park

der Zoo zoo

die Aktivitäten • activites

das Radfahren
cycling

das Jogging
jogging

das Skateboardfahren
skateboarding

das Inlinerfahren
rollerblading

der Reitweg
bridle path

**der Pick-
nickkorb**
hamper

das Vogelbeobachten
bird-watching

das Reiten
horseback riding

das Wandern
hiking

das Picknick
picnic

der Spielplatz • playground

der Sandkasten
sandbox

das Planschbecken
wading pool

die Schaukel
swings

die Wippe | seesaw

die Rutsche
slide

das Klettergerüst
climbing frame

der Strand • beach

das Hotel	der Sonnenschirm	das Strandhäuschen	der Sand	die Welle	das Meer
hotel	beach umbrella	beach hut	sand	wave	sea

die Strandtasche | beach bag

der Bikini | bikini

sonnenbaden | sunbathe (v)

der
Rettungsschwimmer
lifeguard

der Rettungsturm
lifeguard tower

der Windschutz
windbreak

die Promenade
boardwalk

der Liegestuhl
deck chair

die Sonnenbrille
sunglasses

der Sonnenhut
sun hat

die Sonnenmilch
suntan lotion

der Sonnenblock
sunblock

der Wasserball
beach ball

der Schwimmreifen
inflatable ring

der Badeanzug
swimsuit

die Schaufel
shovel

der Eimer
pail

die Sandburg
sandcastle

die Muschel
shell

das Strandtuch
beach towel

das Camping • camping

die Toiletten
restrooms

die Mülleimer
waste disposal

die Duschen
shower block

der Stromanschluss
electric hookup

das Überdach
flysheet

der Hering
tent peg

der Campingplatz
campground

die
Zeltspannleine
guy rope

der
Wohnwagen
camper

Vokabular • vocabulary

zelten
camp (v)

Zeltplätze frei
sites available

voll
full

**die
Campingplatzverwaltung**
site manager's office

der Zeltplatz
site

die Zeltstange
tent pole

das Faltbett
camp bed

**ein Zelt
aufschlagen**
pitch a tent (v)

die Picknickbank
picnic bench

die Hängematte
hammock

das Wohnmobil
camper van

der Anhänger
trailer

die Holzkohle
charcoal

der Feueranzünder
firelighter

ein Feuer machen
light a fire (v)

das Lagerfeuer
campfire

das Gestänge
frame

der Zeltboden
groundsheet

der Rucksack
backpack

die Thermos
flasche
vacuum flask

die Wasserflasche
water bottle

das Zelt
tent

der Insektenspray
insect repellent

die Taschenlampe
flashlight

das Moskitonetz
mosquito net

die Thermowäsche
thermals

die Wanderschuhe
walking boots

die Regenhaut
rain gear

der Schlafsack
sleeping bag

die Schlafmatte
sleeping mat

der Gasbrenner
camping stove

der Grill
barbecue grill

die Luftmatratze | air mattress

die Privatunterhaltung • home entertainment

die DVD-Platte
DVD

der Discman
personal CD player

der Minidiskrekorder
mini disc recorder

der MP3-Spieler
MP3 player

der DVD-Spieler
DVD player

der Plattenspieler
record player

der CD-Spieler
CD player

die Box
speaker

das Radio
radio

der Verstärker
amplifier

der Ständer
speaker stand

die Kopfhörer
headphones

das Rack
stand

die Hi-Fi-Anlage
stereo system

die Videokassette
videotape

der
Bildschirm
screen

die
Okularmuschel
eyecup

der Videorekorder
video recorder

der Camcorder
camcorder

die Satellitenschüssel
satellite dish

der Breitbildfernseher
widescreen television

das Pult
console

der Vorlauf
fast-forward

die Pause
pause

die Aufnahme
record

die Lautstärke
volume

der Steuerhebel
controller

der Rücklauf
rewind

der Stop
stop

das Abspielen
play

die Fernbedienung
remote control

das Videospiel | video game

Vokabular • vocabulary

die CD-Platte CD	**der Spielfilm** feature film	**das Kabelfernsehen** cable television	**digital** digital	**stereo** stereo
die Kassette cassette tape	**die Werbung** advertisement	**das Programm** program	**fernsehen** watch television (v)	**das Radio einstellen** tune the radio (v)
der Kassettenrekorder cassette player	**der Pay-Kanal** pay-per-view channel	**den Kanal wechseln** change channels (v)	**den Fernseher einschalten** turn on the television (v)	**den Fernseher abschalten** turn off the television (v)

---

die Fotografie • photography

der Zähler
frame counter

der Blitz
flash

der Blendenregler
aperture dial

der Filter
filter

der Auslöser
shutter release

die Schutzkappe
lens cap

die Zeiteinstellscheibe
shutter-speed dial

die Linse
lens

die Spiegelreflexkamera | SLR camera

der Elektronenblitz
flash gun

der Belichtungsmesser
light meter

das Zoom
zoom lens

das Stativ
tripod

die Fotoapparattypen • types of camera

die Digitalkamera
digital camera

die Kamera für APS-Film
APS camera

die Sofortbildkamera
instant camera

die Einwegkamera
disposable camera

fotografieren • photograph (v)

die
Filmspule
film roll

der Film
film

einstellen
focus (v)

entwickeln
develop (v)

das Negativ
negative

quer
landscape

hoch
portrait

das Foto | photograph

das Fotoalbum
photo album

der Fotorahmen
picture frame

die Probleme • problems

unterbelichtet
underexposed

überbelichtet
overexposed

unscharf
out of focus

die Rotfärbung der Augen
red eye

Vokabular • vocabulary

der Bildsucher viewfinder	**der Abzug** print
die Kameratasche camera case	**matt** mat
die Belichtung exposure	**hochglanz** gloss
die Dunkelkammer darkroom	**die Vergrößerung** enlargement

Könnten Sie diesen Film entwickeln lassen?
I'd like this film processed

die Spiele • games

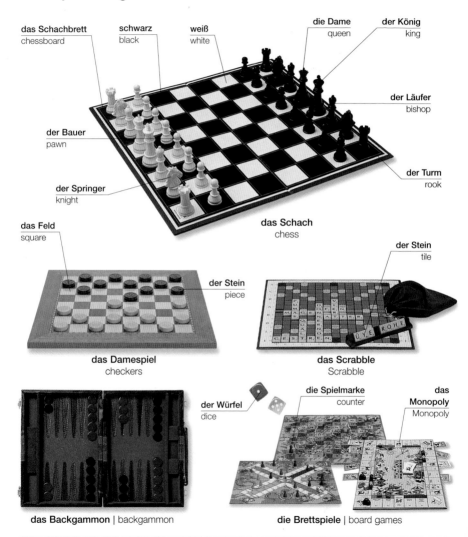

das Schachbrett
chessboard

schwarz
black

weiß
white

die Dame
queen

der König
king

der Läufer
bishop

der Bauer
pawn

der Springer
knight

der Turm
rook

das Feld
square

das Schach
chess

der Stein
tile

der Stein
piece

das Damespiel
checkers

das Scrabble
Scrabble

der Würfel
dice

die Spielmarke
counter

das
Monopoly
Monopoly

das Backgammon | backgammon

die Brettspiele | board games

die Dartscheibe
dartboard

das Bull's Eye
bullseye

das Briefmarkensammeln
stamp collecting

das Puzzle
jigsaw puzzle

das Domino
dominoes

das Darts
darts

der Joker
joker

der Bube
jack

die Dame
queen

der König
king

das Ass
ace

die Karten
cards

das Karo
diamond

das Pik
spade

das Herz
heart

das Kreuz
club

mischen | shuffle (v)

geben | deal (v)

Vokabular • vocabulary

der Zug move	**gewinnen** win (v)	**der Verlierer** loser	**das Bridge** bridge	**der Punkt** point	**Wer ist dran?** Whose turn is it?
spielen play (v)	**der Gewinner** winner	**das Spiel** game	**das Poker** poker	**die Farbe** suit	**Du bist dran.** It's your move.
der Spieler player	**verlieren** lose (v)	**die Wette** bet	**das Kartenspiel** deck of cards	**das Spielergebnis** score	**Würfle.** Roll the dice.

---

das Kunsthandwerk 1 • arts and crafts 1

die Künstlerin
artist

das Gemälde
painting

die Staffelei
easel

die Leinwand
canvas

der Pinsel
brush

die Palette
palette

die Malerei | painting

die Farben • paints

die Ölfarben
oil paints

die Aquarellfarbe
watercolor paint

die Pastellstifte
pastels

die Acrylfarbe
acrylic paint

die Plakatfarbe
poster paint

die Farben • colours

rot red	**blau** blue	**gelb** yellow	**grün** green
orange orange	**lila** purple	**weiß** white	**schwarz** black
grau gray	**rosa** pink	**braun** brown	**indigoblau** indigo

andere Kunstfertigkeiten • other crafts

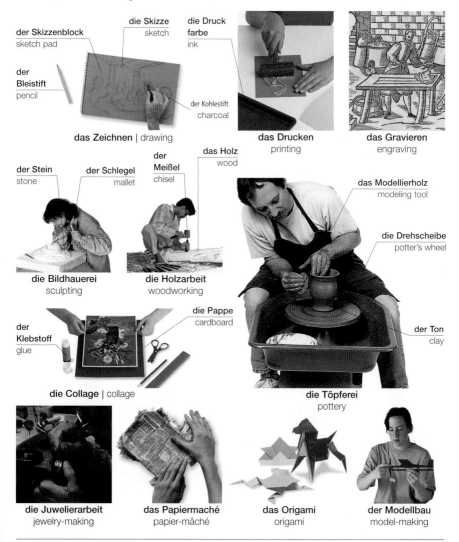

der Skizzenblock
sketch pad

der
Bleistift
pencil

die Skizze
sketch

der Kohlestift
charcoal

das Zeichnen | drawing

die Druck
farbe
ink

das Drucken
printing

das Gravieren
engraving

der Stein
stone

der Schlegel
mallet

der
Meißel
chisel

das Holz
wood

die Bildhauerei
sculpting

die Holzarbeit
woodworking

das Modellierholz
modeling tool

die Drehscheibe
potter's wheel

der Ton
clay

der
Klebstoff
glue

die Pappe
cardboard

die Collage | collage

die Töpferei
pottery

die Juwelierarbeit
jewelry-making

das Papiermaché
papier-mâché

das Origami
origami

der Modellbau
model-making

das Kunsthandwerk 2 • arts and crafts 2

der Fadenleiter
thread guide

der Spuler
thread reel

die Nadel
needle

das Handrad
balance wheel

der Stoffdrücker
presser foot

der Stichwähler
stitch selector

die Stichplatte
needle plate

die Nähmaschine | sewing machine

die Schere
scissors

das Schnittmuster
pattern

das Nadelkissen
pincushion

die Stecknadel
pin

das Zentimetermaß
tape measure

der Stoff
material

der Nähkorb | sewing basket

das Garn
thread

die Öse
eye

die Spule
bobbin

der Haken
hook

der Fingerhut
thimble

die Schneiderkreide
tailor's chalk

die Schneiderpuppe
tailor's dummy

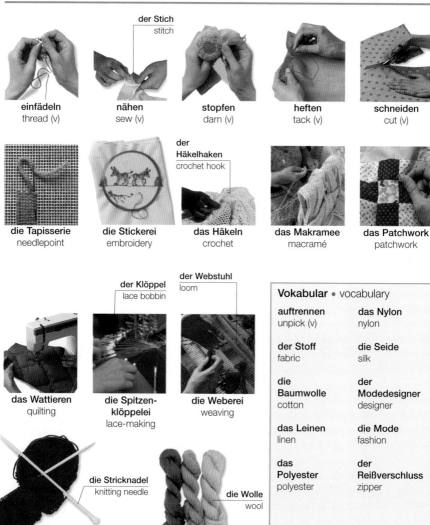

der Stich
stitch

einfädeln
thread (v)

nähen
sew (v)

stopfen
darn (v)

heften
tack (v)

schneiden
cut (v)

die Tapisserie
needlepoint

die Stickerei
embroidery

der Häkelhaken
crochet hook

das Häkeln
crochet

das Makramee
macramé

das Patchwork
patchwork

der Klöppel
lace bobbin

der Webstuhl
loom

das Wattieren
quilting

die Spitzen-klöppelei
lace-making

die Weberei
weaving

die Stricknadel
knitting needle

die Wolle
wool

das Stricken | knitting

der Strang | skein

Vokabular • vocabulary

auftrennen unpick (v)	**das Nylon** nylon
der Stoff fabric	**die Seide** silk
die Baumwolle cotton	**der Modedesigner** designer
das Leinen linen	**die Mode** fashion
das Polyester polyester	**der Reißverschluss** zipper

die Umwelt
environment

der Weltraum • space

der Merkur
Mercury

die Erde
Earth

der Mars
Mars

der Jupiter
Jupiter

der Neptun
Neptune

der Uranus
Uranus

der Pluto
Pluto

die Venus
Venus

der Mond
Moon

die Sonne
Sun

das Sonnensystem
Saturn

das Sonnensystem | solar system

die Galaxie
galaxy

der Nebelfleck
nebula

der Asteroid
asteroid

der Schweif
tail

der Stern
star

der Komet
comet

vokabular • vocabulary

der Planet planet	das Universum universe	der Vollmond full moon
der Meteor meteor	die Umlaufbahn orbit	der Neumond new moon
die Schwerkraft gravity	das schwarze Loch black hole	die Mondsichel crescent moon

die Finsternis | eclipse

deutsch • english

die Raumforschung • space exploration

der Radar
radar

die Raumfähre
space shuttle

die Steuerrakete
thruster

die Besatzungsluke
crew hatch

der Raumanzug
space suit

der Booster
booster

der Astronaut | astronaut

die Mondfähre | lunar module

die Abschussrampe
launch pad

der Abschuss
launch

der Satellit
satellite

die Raumstation
space station

die Astronomie • astronomy

das Sternbild
constellation

das Fernglas
binoculars

das Teleskop
telescope

das Stativ
tripod

die Erde • Earth

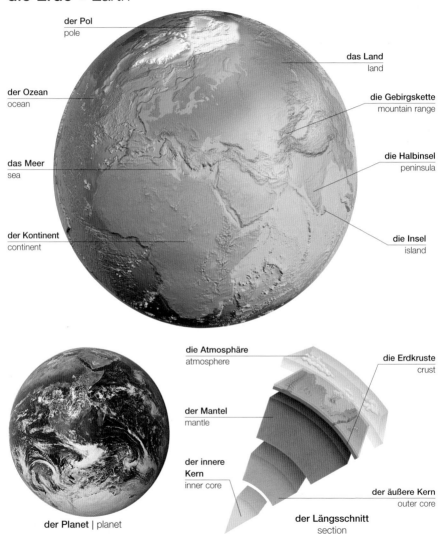

der Pol
pole

das Land
land

der Ozean
ocean

die Gebirgskette
mountain range

das Meer
sea

die Halbinsel
peninsula

der Kontinent
continent

die Insel
island

die Atmosphäre
atmosphere

die Erdkruste
crust

der Mantel
mantle

der innere
Kern
inner core

der äußere Kern
outer core

der Planet | planet

der Längsschnitt
section

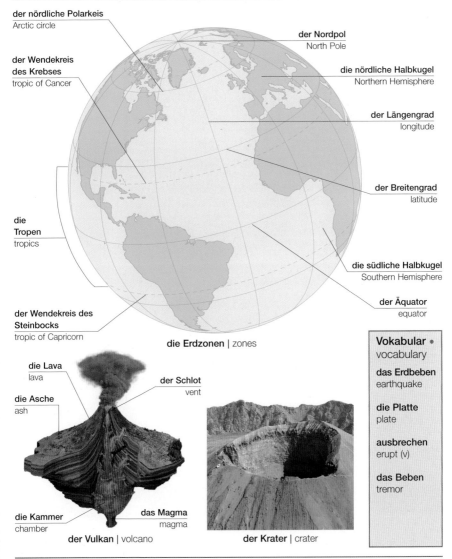

der nördliche Polarkeis
Arctic circle

der Wendekreis des Krebses
tropic of Cancer

der Nordpol
North Pole

die nördliche Halbkugel
Northern Hemisphere

der Längengrad
longitude

der Breitengrad
latitude

die Tropen
tropics

die südliche Halbkugel
Southern Hemisphere

der Äquator
equator

der Wendekreis des Steinbocks
tropic of Capricorn

die Erdzonen | zones

die Lava
lava

der Schlot
vent

die Asche
ash

die Kammer
chamber

das Magma
magma

der Vulkan | volcano

der Krater | crater

Vokabular • vocabulary

das Erdbeben
earthquake

die Platte
plate

ausbrechen
erupt (v)

das Beben
tremor

die Landschaft • landscape

der Berg
mountain

der Hang
slope

das Ufer
bank

der Fluss
river

die Strom schnellen
rapids

die Felsen
rocks

der Gletscher
glacier

das Tal | valley

der Hügel
hill

das Plateau
plateau

die Schlucht
gorge

die Höhle
cave

die Ebene | plain

die Wüste | desert

der Wald | forest

der Wald | wood

der Regenwald
rainforest

der Sumpf
swamp

die Wiese label
meadow

das Grasland
grassland

der Wasserfall
waterfall

der Bach
stream

der See
lake

der Geysir
geyser

die Küste
coast

die Klippe
cliff

das Korallenriff
coral reef

die Flussmündung
estuary

das Wetter • weather

die Exosphäre
exosphere

das Polarlicht
aurora

die Thermosphäre
thermosphere

die Mesosphäre
mesosphere

die Ionosphäre
ionosphere

die Ultraviolettstrahlen
ultraviolet rays

die Stratosphäre
stratosphere

die Troposphäre
troposphere

die Ozonschicht
ozone layer

die Atmosphäre | atmosphere

der Sonnenschein
sunshine

der Wind
wind

Vokabular • vocabulary

der Schneeregen sleet	**der Schauer** shower	**heiß** hot	**trocken** dry	**windig** windy	**Mir ist heiß/kalt.** I'm hot/cold.
der Hagel hail	**sonnig** sunny	**kalt** cold	**nass** wet	**der Sturm** gale	**Es regnet.** It's raining.
der Donner thunder	**bewölkt** cloudy	**warm** warm	**feucht** humid	**die Temperatur** temperature	**Es sind … Grad.** It's … degrees.

die Wolke
cloud

der Regen
rain

der Blitz
lightning

das Gewitter
storm

der feine Nebel
mist

der dichte Nebel
fog

der Regenbogen
rainbow

der Eiszapfen
icicle

der Schnee
snow

der Raureif
frost

das Eis
ice

der Frost
freeze

der Hurrikan
hurricane

der Tornado
tornado

der Monsun
monsoon

die Überschwemmung
flood

das Gestein • rocks

eruptiv • igneous

der Granit
granite

der Obsidian
obsidian

der Basalt
basalt

der Bimsstein
pumice

sedimentär • sedimentary

der Sandstein
sandstone

der Kalkstein
limestone

die Kreide
chalk

der Feuerstein
flint

das Konglomerat
conglomerate

die Kohle
coal

metamorph • metamorphic

der Schiefer
slate

der Glimmers
schist

der Gneis
gneiss

der Marmor
marble

die Schmucksteine • gems

der Rubin
ruby

der Aquamarin
aquamarine

der Amethyst
amethyst

der Diamant
diamond

der Jade
jade

der Jett
jet

der Smaragd
emerald

der Opal
opal

der Saphir
sapphire

der Mondstein
moonstone

der Granat
garnet

der Topas
topaz

der Turmalin
tourmaline

die Mineralien • minerals

der Quarz	der Glimmer	der Schwefel	der Hämatit	der Kalzit
quartz	mica	sulfur	hematite	calcite

der Malachit	der Türkis	der Onyx	der Achat	der Graphit
malachite	turquoise	onyx	agate	graphite

die Metalle • metals

das Gold	das Silber	das Platin	das Nickel	das Eisen
gold	silver	platinum	nickel	iron

das Kupfer	das Zinn	das Aluminium	das Quecksilber	das Zink
copper	tin	aluminum	mercury	zinc

die Tiere 1 • animals 1
die Säugetiere • mammals

die Schnurrhaare
whiskers

der Schwanz
tail

das Kaninchen
rabbit

der Hamster
hamster

die Maus
mouse

die Ratte
rat

der Igel
hedgehog

das Eichhörnchen
squirrel

die Fledermaus
bat

der Waschbär
raccoon

der Fuchs
fox

der Wolf
wolf

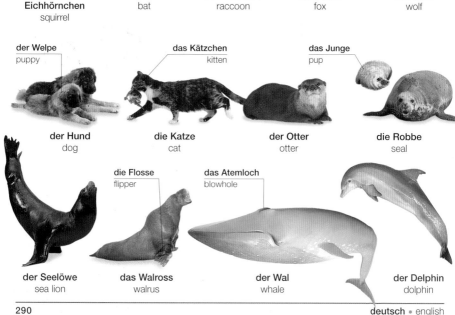

der Welpe
puppy

das Kätzchen
kitten

das Junge
pup

der Hund
dog

die Katze
cat

der Otter
otter

die Robbe
seal

die Flosse
flipper

das Atemloch
blowhole

der Seelöwe
sea lion

das Walross
walrus

der Wal
whale

der Delphin
dolphin

das Geweih
antler

die Mähne
mane

der Höcker
hump

der Huf
hoof

der Hirsch
deer

das Zebra
zebra

die Giraffe
giraffe

das Kamel
camel

der Rüssel
trunk

der Stoßzahn
tusk

das Horn
horn

das Nilpferd
hippopotamus

der Elefant
elephant

das Nashorn
rhinoceros

der Tiger
tiger

die Mähne
mane

der Löwe
lion

der Affe
monkey

der Gorilla
gorilla

der Koalabär
koala

der Beutel
pouch

der Pandabär
panda

die Klaue
claw

das Känguru
kangaroo

der Bär
bear

der Eisbär
polar bear

die Tiere 2 • animals 2
die Vögel • birds

der Schwanz
tail

der Kanarienvogel
canary

der Spatz
sparrow

der Kolibri
hummingbird

die Schwalbe
swallow

die Krähe
crow

die Taube
pigeon

der Specht
woodpecker

der Falke
falcon

die Eule
owl

die Möwe
gull

der Adler
eagle

der Pelikan
pelican

der Flamingo
flamingo

der Storch
stork

der Kranich
crane

der Pinguin
penguin

der Strauß
ostrich

die Reptilien • reptiles

die Gans | goose

der Schwan
swan

die Schuppen
scales

der Alligator
alligator

der Pfau
peacock

der Fasan
pheasant

die Eidechse
lizard

der Leguan
iguana

der Panzer
shell

der Truthahn
turkey

die Wasserschildkröte
turtle

die Schildkröte
tortoise

die Schlange
snake

der Schnabel
bill

die Feder
feather

der
Flügel
wing

die Schnauze
snout

der Kakadu
cockatoo

die Kralle
claw

der Papagei
parrot

das Krokodil
crocodile

die Tiere 3 • animals 3
die Amphibien • amphibians

| **der Frosch**
frog | **die Kröte**
toad | **die Kaulquappe**
tadpole | **der Salamander**
salamander |

die Fische • fish

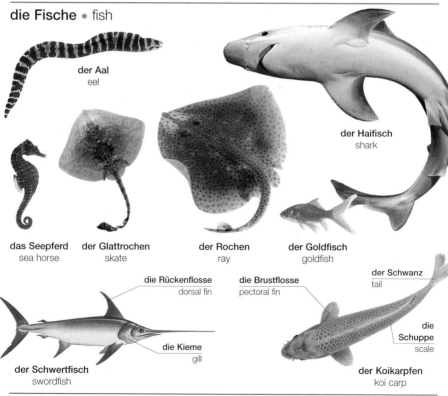

der Aal
eel

der Haifisch
shark

das Seepferd
sea horse

der Glattrochen
skate

der Rochen
ray

der Goldfisch
goldfish

die Rückenflosse
dorsal fin

die Brustflosse
pectoral fin

der Schwanz
tail

die Kieme
gill

die Schuppe
scale

der Schwertfisch
swordfish

der Koikarpfen
koi carp

die Wirbellosen • invertebrates

die Ameise
ant

die Termite
termite

die Biene
bee

die Wespe
wasp

der Käfer
beetle

der Kakerlak
cockroach

die Motte
moth

der Fühler
antenna

der Schmetterling
butterfly

der Kokon
cocoon

die Raupe
caterpillar

die Grille
cricket

die Heuschrecke
grasshopper

die Gottesanbeterin
praying mantis

der
Stachel
sting

der Skorpion
scorpion

**der
Tausendfüßer**
centipede

die Libelle
dragonfly

die Fliege
fly

die Stechmücke
mosquito

der Marienkäfer
ladybug

die Spinne
spider

**die
Wegschnecke**
slug

die Schnecke
snail

der Wurm
worm

der Seestern
starfish

die Muschel
mussel

der Krebs
crab

der Hummer
lobster

der Krake
octopus

der Tintenfisch
squid

die Qualle
jellyfish

die Pflanzen • plants

der Baum • tree

der Ast
branch

das Blatt
leaf

der Zweig
twig

die Rinde
bark

die Weide
willow

die Wurzel
root

der Stamm
trunk

die Eiche
oak

die Pappel
poplar

der Eukalyptus
eucalyptus

die Lärche
larch

die Buche
beech

die Birke
birch

die Kiefer
pine

die Zeder
cedar

der Ahorn
maple

die Ulme
elm

die Linde
lime

die Stechpalme
holly

die Beere
berry

die Palme
palm

die blühende Pflanze • flowering plant

die Blüte
flower

das
Staubgefäß
stamen

das
Blütenblatt
petal

der Kelch
calyx

der Stängel
stalk

der Stiel
stem

die Knospe
bud

der Hahnenfuß
buttercup

das
Gänseblümchen
daisy

die Distel
thistle

der Löwenzahn
dandelion

das Heidekraut
heather

der
Klatschmohn
poppy

der Fingerhut
foxglove

das Geißblatt
honeysuckle

die
Sonnenblume
sunflower

der Klee
clover

die
Sternhyazinthen
bluebells

die
Schlüsselblume
primrose

die Lupinen
lupines

die Nessel
nettle

die Stadt • town

die Straße
street

die Bordkante
curb

die Straßenecke
street corner

der Laden
shop

die Kreuzung
intersection

die Einbahn
straße
one-way
system

der
Bürgersteig
sidewalk

das
Bürogebäude
office building

der
Wohnblock
apartment
building

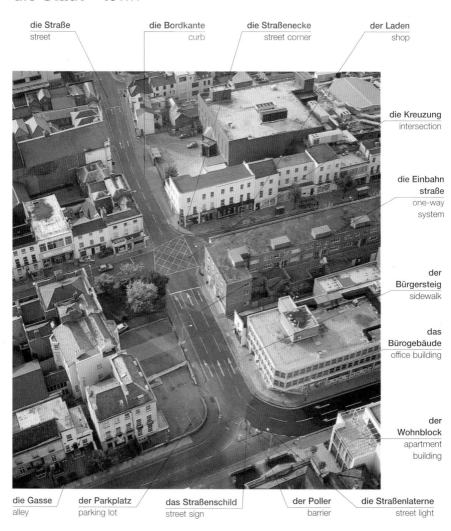

die Gasse
alley

der Parkplatz
parking lot

das Straßenschild
street sign

der Poller
barrier

die Straßenlaterne
street light

die Gebäude • buildings

das Rathaus
town hall

die Bibliothek
library

das Kino
movie theater

das Theater
theater

die Universität
university

der Wolkenkratzer
skyscraper

die Wohngegend • areas

das Industriegebiet
industrial park

die Stadt
city

der Vorort
suburb

das Dorf
village

die Schule
school

Vokabular • vocabulary

die Fußgängerzone pedestrian zone	**die Seitenstraße** side street	**der Kanalschacht** utility cover	**der Rinnstein** gutter	**die Kirche** church
die Allee avenue	**der Platz** square	**die Bushaltestelle** bus stop	**die Fabrik** factory	**der Kanal** drain

---

die Architektur • architecture

die Gebäude und Strukturen • buildings and structures

die **Kreuzblume**
finial

der **Mauerturm**
turret

die **Turmspitze**
spire

der **Burggraben**
moat

der **Wolkenkratzer**
skyscraper

die **Burg**
castle

der **Giebel**
gable

die **Kuppel**
dome

der **Turm**
tower

die **Kirche**
church

die **Moschee**
mosque

das **Gewölbe**
vault

der **Tempel**
temple

die **Synagoge**
synagogue

das **Gesims**
cornice

der **Staudamm**
dam

die **Brücke**
bridge

die **Säule**
pillar

die **Kathedrale** | cathedral

die Baustile • styles

gotisch
gothic

der Architrav
architrave

Renaissance
Renaissance

barock
baroque

der Bogen
arch

der Fries
frieze

der Chor
choir

Rokoko
rococo

das Giebeldreieck
pediment

der Strebepfeiler
buttress

klassizistisch
neoclassical

der Jugendstil
Art Nouveau

Art-déco
Art Deco

die Information
reference

die Uhrzeit • time

der Minutenzeiger
minute hand

der Stundenzeiger
hour hand

die Uhr
clock

Vokabular • vocabulary

die Stunde hour	**jetzt** now	**zwanzig Minuten** twenty minutes
die Minute minute	**später** later	**vierzig Minuten** forty minutes
die Sekunde second	**eine halbe stunde** half an hour	**eine Viertelstunde** a quarter of an hour

Wie spät ist es?
What time is it?

Es ist drei Uhr.
It's three o'clock.

fünf nach eins
five after one

zehn nach eins
ten after one

Viertel nach eins
quarter after one

zwanzig nach eins
twenty after one

der Sekundenzeiger
second hand

fünf vor halb zwei
twenty-five after one

ein Uhr dreißig
one thirty

fünf nach halb zwei
twenty-five to two

zwanzig vor zwei
twenty to two

Viertel vor zwei
quarter to two

zehn vor zwei
ten to two

fünf vor zwei
five to two

zwei Uhr
two o'clock

die Nacht und der Tag • night and day

die Mitternacht
midnight

der Sonnenaufgang
sunrise

die Morgendämmerung
dawn

der Morgen
morning

der Sonnenuntergang
sunset

der Mittag
noon

die Abenddämmerung
dusk

der Abend
evening

der Nachmittag
afternoon

Vokabular • vocabulary

früh early	**Du bist früh.** You're early.	**Sei bitte pünktlich.** Please be on time.	**Wann ist es zu Ende?** What time does it end?
pünktlich on time	**Du hast dich verspätet.** You're late.	**Bis später.** I'll see you later.	**Wie lange dauert es?** How long will it last?
spät late	**Ich werde bald dort sein.** I'll be there soon.	**Wann fängt es an?** What time does it start?	**Es ist schon spät.** It's getting late.

der Kalender • calendar

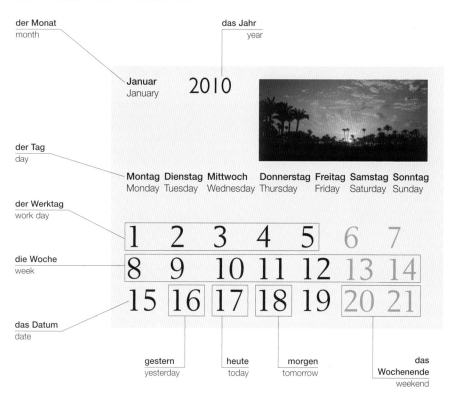

der Monat
month

das Jahr
year

Januar
January

2010

der Tag
day

Montag	**Dienstag**	**Mittwoch**	**Donnerstag**	**Freitag**	**Samstag**	**Sonntag**
Monday	Tuesday	Wednesday	Thursday	Friday	Saturday	Sunday

der Werktag
work day

die Woche
week

das Datum
date

1	2	3	4	5	6	7
8	9	10	11	12	13	14
15	16	17	18	19	20	21

gestern
yesterday

heute
today

morgen
tomorrow

das Wochenende
weekend

Vokabular • vocabulary

Januar	**März**	**Mai**	**Juli**	**September**	**November**
January	March	May	July	September	November
Februar	**April**	**Juni**	**August**	**Oktober**	**Dezember**
February	April	June	August	October	December

die Jahre • years

1900   **neunzehnhundert** • nineteen hundred

1901   **neunzehnhunderteins** • nineteen hundred and one

1910   **neunzehnhundertzehn** • nineteen ten

2000   **zweitausend** • two thousand

2001   **zweitausendeins** • two thousand and one

die Jahreszeiten • seasons

der Frühling
spring

der Sommer
summer

der Herbst
fall

der Winter
winter

Vokabular • vocabulary

das Jahrhundert
century

das Jahrzehnt
decade

das Jahrtausend
millennium

diese Woche
this week

letzte Woche
last week

nächste Woche
next week

vorgestern
the day before yesterday

übermorgen
the day after tomorrow

wöchentlich
weekly

monatlich
monthly

jährlich
annual

Welches Datum haben wir heute?
What's the date today?

Heute ist der siebte Februar zweitausendzwei.
It's February seventh, two thousand and two.

die Zahlen • numbers

0	**null** • zero		20	**zwanzig** • twenty
1	**eins** • one		21	**einundzwanzig** • twenty-one
2	**zwei** • two		22	**zweiundzwanzig** • twenty-two
3	**drei** • three		30	**dreißig** • thirty
4	**vier** • four		40	**vierzig** • forty
5	**fünf** • five		50	**fünfzig** • fifty
6	**sechs** • six		60	**sechzig** • sixty
7	**sieben** • seven		70	**siebzig** • seventy
8	**acht** • eight		80	**achtzig** • eighty
9	**neun** • nine		90	**neunzig** • ninety
10	**zehn** • ten		100	**hundert** • one hundred
11	**elf** • eleven		110	**hundertzehn** • one hundred and ten
12	**zwölf** • twelve		200	**zweihundert** • two hundred
13	**dreizehn** • thirteen		300	**dreihundert** • three hundred
14	**vierzehn** • fourteen		400	**vierhundert** • four hundred
15	**fünfzehn** • fifteen		500	**fünfhundert** • five hundred
16	**sechzehn** • sixteen		600	**sechshundert** • six hundred
17	**siebzehn** • seventeen		700	**siebenhundert** • seven hundred
18	**achtzehn** • eighteen		800	**achthundert** • eight hundred
19	**neunzehn** • nineteen		900	**neunhundert** • nine hundred

1,000	**tausend** • one thousand	
10,000	**zehntausend** • ten thousand	
20,000	**zwanzigtausend** • twenty thousand	
50,000	**fünfzigtausend** • fifty thousand	
55,500	**fünfundfünfzigtausend-fünfhundert** • fifty-five thousand five hundred	
100,000	**hunderttausend** • one hundred thousand	
1,000,000	**eine Million** • one million	
1,000,000,000	**eine Milliarde** • one billion	

erster first   **zweiter** second   **dritter** third

vierter • fourth

fünfter • fifth

sechster • sixth

siebter • seventh

achter • eighth

neunter • ninth

zehnter • tenth

elfter • eleventh

zwölfter • twelfth

dreizehnter • thirteenth

vierzehnter • fourteenth

fünfzehnter • fifteenth

sechzehnter • sixteenth

siebzehnter • seventeenth

achtzehnter • eighteenth

neunzehnter • nineteenth

zwanzigster • twentieth

einundzwanzigster • twenty-first

zweiundzwanzigster • twenty-second

dreiundzwanzigster • twenty-third

dreißigster • thirtieth

vierzigster • fortieth

fünfzigster • fiftieth

sechzigster • sixtieth

siebzigster • seventieth

achtzigster • eightieth

neunzigster • ninetieth

hundertster • hundredth

die Maße und Gewichte • weights and measures

die Fläche • area

der Quadratfuß	der Quadratmeter
square foot	square meter

die Entfernung • distance

der Kilometer	die Meile
kilometer	mile

die Waagschale
pan

das Pfund
pound

die Unze
ounce

das Kilogramm
kilogram

das Gramm
gram

die Waage | scale

Vokabular • vocabulary

das Yard	die Tonne	messen
yard	ton	measure (v)
der Meter	das Milligramm	wiegen
meter	milligram	weigh (v)

die Länge • length

der Fuß
foot

der Millimeter	der Zentimeter	der Zoll
millimeter	centimeter	inch

das Fassungsvermögen • capacity

der halbe Liter
half-liter

das Pint
pint

das Volumen
volume

Vokabular •
vocabulary

die Gallone
gallon

das Quart
quart

der Liter
liter

der Milliliter
milliliter

der Messbecher
measuring cup

das Flüssigkeitsmaß
liquid measure

der Behälter • container

der Beutel
bag

die Tüte
carton

das Päckchen
packet

die Flasche
bottle

die Dose
can

die Dose | tub

das Glas | jar

die Dose | tin

die Spritze
spray bottle

das Stück
bar

die Tube
tube

die Rolle
roll

das Päckchen
pack

die Sprühdose
spray can

die Weltkarte • world map

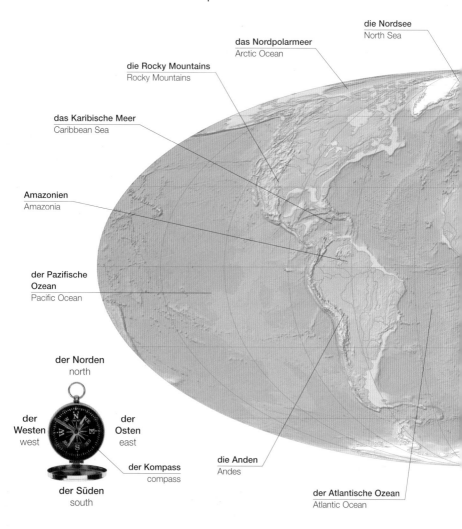

die Nordsee
North Sea

das Nordpolarmeer
Arctic Ocean

die Rocky Mountains
Rocky Mountains

das Karibische Meer
Caribbean Sea

Amazonien
Amazonia

der Pazifische
Ozean
Pacific Ocean

der Norden
north

**der
Westen**
west

**der
Osten**
east

der Kompass
compass

der Süden
south

die Anden
Andes

der Atlantische Ozean
Atlantic Ocean

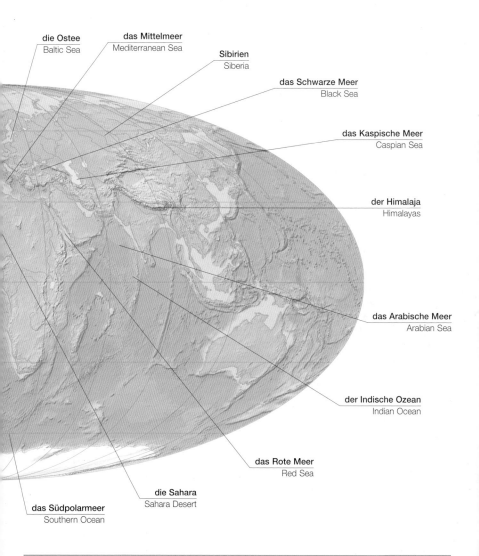

die Ostee
Baltic Sea

das Mittelmeer
Mediterranean Sea

Sibirien
Siberia

das Schwarze Meer
Black Sea

das Kaspische Meer
Caspian Sea

der Himalaja
Himalayas

das Arabische Meer
Arabian Sea

der Indische Ozean
Indian Ocean

das Rote Meer
Red Sea

die Sahara
Sahara Desert

das Südpolarmeer
Southern Ocean

Nord- und Mittelamerika • North and Central America

Hawaii
Hawaii

1 **Alaska** • Alaska
2 **Kanada** • Canada
3 **Grönland** • Greenland
4 **die Vereinigten Staten**
   • United States of America
5 **Mexiko** • Mexico
6 **Guatemala** • Guatemala
7 **Belize** • Belize
8 **El Salvador** • El Salvador
9 **Honduras** • Honduras
10 **Nicaragua** • Nicaragua
11 **Costa Rica** • Costa Rica
12 **Panama** • Panama
13 **Kuba** • Cuba
14 **die Bahamas** • Bahamas
15 **Jamaika** • Jamaica
16 **Haiti** • Haiti
17 **die Dominikanische Republik**
   • Dominican Republic
18 **Puerto Rico** • Puerto Rico
19 **Barbados** • Barbados
20 **Trinidad und Tobago** • Trinidad and Tobago
21 **Saint Kitts und Nevis** • St. Kitts and Nevis

22 **Antigua und Barbuda** • Antigua and Barbuda
23 **Dominica** • Dominica
24 **Saint Lucia** • St. Lucia
25 **Saint Vinzent und die Grenadinen**
   • St. Vincent and The Grenadines
26 **Grenada** • Grenada

Südamerika • South America

1 **Venezuela** • Venezuela

2 **Kolumbien** • Colombia

3 **Ecuador** • Ecuador

4 **Peru** • Peru

5 **die Galapagosinseln**
• Galapagos Islands

6 **Guyana** • Guyana

7 **Suriname** • Suriname

8 **Französisch-Guayana**
• French Guiana

9 **Brasilien** • Brazil

10 **Bolivien** • Bolivia

11 **Chile** • Chile

12 **Argentinien** • Argentina

13 **Paraguay** • Paraguay

14 **Uruguay** • Uruguay

15 **die Falklandinseln**
• Falkland Islands

Vokabular • vocabulary

der Staat	die Kolonie	die Zone
state	colony	zone
das Land	die Provinz	die Region
country	province	region
die Nation	das Territorium	der Bezirk
nation	territory	district
der Kontinent	das Fürstentum	die Hauptstadt
continent	principality	capital

Europa • Europe

1 **Irland** • Ireland

2 **das Vereinigte Königreich**
   • United Kingdom

3 **Portugal** • Portugal

4 **Spanien** • Spain

5 **die Balearen**
   • Balearic Islands

6 **Andorra** • Andorra

7 **Frankreich** • France

8 **Belgien** • Belgium

9 **die Niederlande**
   • Netherlands

10 **Luxemburg** • Luxembourg

11 **Deutschland** • Germany

12 **Dänemark** • Denmark

13 **Norwegen** • Norway

14 **Schweden** • Sweden

15 **Finnland** • Finland

16 **Estland** • Estonia

17 **Lettland** • Latvia

18 **Litauen** • Lithuania

19 **Kaliningrad**
   • Kaliningrad

20 **Polen** • Poland

21 **die Tschechische
   Republik**
   • Czech Republic

22 **Österreich** • Austria

23 **Liechtenstein**
   • Liechtenstein

24 **die Schweiz**
   • Switzerland

25 **Italien** • Italy

26 **Monaco**
   • Monaco

27 **Korsika** • Corsica

28 **Sardinien** • Sardinia

29 **San Marino** • San Marino

30 **die Vatikanstadt**
   • Vatican City

31 **Sizilien** • Sicily

32 **Malta** • Malta

33 **Slowenien** • Slovenia

34 **Kroatien** • Croatia

35 **Ungarn** • Hungary

36 **die Slowakei** • Slovakia

37 **die Ukraine** • Ukraine

38 **Weißrussland** • Belarus

39 **Moldawien** • Moldova

40 **Rumänien** • Romania

41 **Serbien** • Serbia

42 **Bosnien und Herzegowina**
   • Bosnia and Herzogovina

43 **Albanien** • Albania

44 **Mazedonien** • Macedonia

45 **Bulgarien** • Bulgaria

46 **Griechenland** • Greece

47 **Kosovo** • Kosovo (disputed)

48 **Montenegro** • Montenegro

Afrika • Africa

1 **Marokko** • Morocco

2 **Westsahara**
• Western Sahara

3 **Mauretanien**
• Mauritania

4 **Senegal** • Senegal

5 **Gambia** • Gambia

6 **Guinea-Bissau**
• Guinea-Bissau

7 **Guinea** • Guinea

8 **Sierra Leone** • Sierra Leone

9 **Liberia** • Liberia

10 **Elfenbeinküste** • Ivory Coast

11 **Burkina Faso** • Burkina Faso

12 **Mali** • Mali

13 **Algerien** • Algeria

14 **Tunesien** • Tunisia

15 **Libyen** • Libya

16 **Niger** • Niger

17 **Ghana** • Ghana

18 **Togo** • Togo

19 **Benin** • Benin

20 **Nigeria** • Nigeria

21 **São Tomé und Príncipe**
• São Tomé and Principe

22 **Äquatorialguinea**
• Equatorial Guinea

23 **Kamerun** • Cameroon

24 **Tschad** • Chad

25 **Ägypten** • Egypt

26 **der Sudan** • Sudan

27 **Eritrea** • Eritrea

28 **Dschibuti** • Djibouti

29 **Äthiopien** • Ethiopia

30 **Somalia** • Somalia

31 **Kenia** • Kenya

32 **Uganda** • Uganda

33 **die Zentralafrikanische
Republik** • Central African
Republic

34 **Gabun** • Gabon

35 **Kongo** • Congo

36 **Kabinda (Angola)**
• Cabinda (Angola)

37 **die Demokratische
Republik Kongo** •
Democratic Republic of
the Congo

38 **Ruanda** • Rwanda

39 **Burundi** • Burundi

40 **Tansania** • Tanzania

41 **Mosambik** • Mozambique

42 **Malawi** • Malawi

43 **Sambia** • Zambia

44 **Angola** • Angola

45 **Namibia** • Namibia

46 **Botsuana** • Botswana

47 **Simbabwe** • Zimbabwe

48 **Südafrika** • South Africa

49 **Lesotho** • Lesotho

50 **Swasiland** • Swaziland

51 **die Komoren** • Comoros

52 **Madagaskar** • Madagascar

53 **Mauritius** • Mauritius

Asien • Asia

1 **die Türkei** • Turkey

2 **Zypern** • Cyprus

3 **die Russische Föderation**
• Russian Federation

4 **Georgien** • Georgia

5 **Armenien** • Armenia

6 **Aserbaidschan** • Azerbaijan

7 **der Iran** • Iran

8 **der Irak** • Iraq

9 **Syrien** • Syria

10 **der Libanon** • Lebanon

11 **Israel** • Israel

12 **Jordanien** • Jordan

13 **Saudi-Arabien**
• Saudi Arabia

14 **Kuwait** • Kuwait

15 **Bahrain** • Bahrain

16 **Katar** • Qatar

17 **Vereinigte Arabische Emirate**
• United Arab Emirates

18 **Oman** • Oman

19 **der Jemen** • Yemen

20 **Kasachstan** • Kazakhstan

21 **Usbekistan** • Uzbekistan

22 **Turkmenistan** • Turkmenistan

23 **Afghanistan** • Afghanistan

24 **Tadschikistan** • Tajikistan

25 **Kirgisistan** • Kyrgyzstan

26 **Pakistan** • Pakistan

27 **Indien** • India

28 **die Malediven** • Maldives

29 **Sri Lanka** • Sri Lanka

30 **China** • China

31 **die Mongolei** • Mongolia

32 **Nordkorea** • North Korea

33 **Südkorea** • South Korea

34 **Japan** • Japan

35 **Nepal** • Nepal

36 **Bhutan** • Bhutan

37 **Bangladesch** • Bangladesh

38 **Birmania (Myanmar)**
• Burma (Myanmar)

39 **Thailand** • Thailand

40 **Laos** • Laos

41 **Vietnam** • Vietnam

42 **Kambodscha** • Cambodia

Australien und Ozeanien •
Australasia

1 **Australien** • Australia
2 **Tasmanien** • Tasmania
3 **Neuseeland** • New Zealand

43 **Malaysia** • Malaysia
44 **Singapur** • Singapore
45 **Indonesien** • Indonesia
46 **Brunei** • Brunei
47 **die Philippinen** • Philippines
48 **Ost-Timor** • East Timor
49 **Papua-Neuguinea**
   • Papua New Guinea
50 **die Salomonen** • Solomon Islands
51 **Vanuatu** • Vanuatu
52 **Fidji** • Fiji

Partikeln und Antonyme • particles and antonyms

zu, nach to	**von, aus** from	**für** for	**zu** toward
über over	**unter** under	**entlang** along	**über** across
vor in front of	**hinter** behind	**mit** with	**ohne** without
auf onto	**in** into	**vor** before	**nach** after
in in	**aus** out	**bis** by	**bis** until
über above	**unter** below	**früh** early	**spät** late
innerhalb inside	**außerhalb** outside	**jetzt** now	**später** later
hinauf up	**hinunter** down	**immer** always	**nie** never
an, bei at	**jenseits** beyond	**oft** often	**selten** rarely
durch through	**um** around	**gestern** yesterday	**morgen** tomorrow
auf on top of	**neben** beside	**erste** first	**letzte** last
zwischen between	**gegenüber** opposite	**jede** every	**etwas** some
nahe near	**weit** far	**gegen** about	**genau** exactly
hier here	**dort** there	**ein wenig** a little	**viel** a lot

groß large	**klein** small	**heiß** hot	**kalt** cold
breit wide	**schmal** narrow	**offen** open	**geschlossen** closed
groß tall	**kurz** short	**voll** full	**leer** empty
hoch high	**niedrig** low	**neu** new	**alt** old
dick thick	**dünn** thin	**hell** light	**dunkel** dark
leicht light	**schwer** heavy	**leicht** easy	**schwer** difficult
hart hard	**weich** soft	**frei** free	**besetzt** occupied
nass wet	**trocken** dry	**stark** strong	**schwach** weak
gut good	**schlecht** bad	**dick** fat	**dünn** thin
schnell fast	**langsam** slow	**jung** young	**alt** old
richtig correct	**falsch** wrong	**besser** better	**schlechter** worse
sauber clean	**schmutzig** dirty	**schwarz** black	**weiß** white
schön beautiful	**hässlich** ugly	**interessant** interesting	**langweilig** boring
teuer expensive	**billig** cheap	**krank** sick	**wohl** well
leise quiet	**laut** noisy	**der Anfang** beginning	**das Ende** end

praktische Redewendungen • useful phrases

wesentliche Redewendungen
• essential phrases

Ja
Yes

Nein
No

Vielleicht
Maybe

Bitte
Please

Danke
Thank you

Bitte sehr
You're welcome

Entschuldigung
Excuse me

Es tut mir Leid
I'm sorry

Nicht
Don't

Okay
OK

In Ordnung
That's fine

Das ist richtig
That's correct

Das ist falsch
That's wrong

Begrüßungen
• greetings

Guten Tag
Hello

Auf Wiedersehen
Goodbye

Guten Morgen
Good morning

Guten Tag
Good afternoon

Guten Abend
Good evening

Gute Nacht
Good night

Wie geht es Ihnen?
How are you?

Ich heiße…
My name is…

Wie heißen Sie?
What is your name?

Wie heißt er/sie?
What is his/her name?

Darf ich… vorstellen
May I introduce…

Das ist…
This is…

Angenehm
Pleased to meet you

Bis später
See you later

Schilder • signs

Touristen-Information
Tourist information

Eingang
Entrance

Ausgang
Exit

Notausgang
Emergency exit

Drücken
Push

Lebensgefahr
Danger

Rauchen verboten
No smoking

Außer Betrieb
Out of order

Öffnungszeiten
Opening times

Eintritt frei
Free admission

Sonderangebot
Special offer

Reduziert
Reduced

Ausverkauf
Sale

Bitte anklopfen
Knock before entering

Betreten des Rasens verboten
Keep off the grass

Hilfe • help

Können Sie mir helfen?
Can you help me?

Ich verstehe nicht
I don't understand

Ich weiß nicht
I don't know

Sprechen Sie Englisch, Französisch…?
Do you speak English, French…?

Ich spreche Englisch, Spanisch…
I speak English, Spanish…

Sprechen Sie bitte langsamer
Please speak more slowly

Schreiben Sie es bitte für mich auf
Please write it down for me

Ich habe… verloren
I have lost…

Richtungsangaben
• directions

Ich habe mich verlaufen
I am lost

Wo ist der/die/das...?
Where is the...?

Wo ist der/die/das nächste...?
Where is the nearest...?

Wo sind die Toiletten?
Where are the restrooms?

Wie komme ich nach...?
How do I get to...?

Nach rechts
To the right

Nach links
To the left

Geradeaus
Straight ahead

Wie weit ist...?
How far is...?

die Verkehrsschilder
• road signs

Langsam fahren
Slow down

Achtung
Caution

Keine Zufahrt
No entry

Umleitung
Detour

Rechts fahren
Keep right

Autobahn
Freeway

Parkverbot
No parking

Sackgasse
No through road

Einbahnstraße
One-way street

Vorfahrt gewähren
Yield

Anlieger frei
Residents only

Baustelle
Road construction

gefährliche Kurve
Dangerous bend

Unterkunft
• accommodation

Haben Sie Zimmer frei?
Do you have any vacancies?

Ich habe ein Zimmer reserviert
I have a reservation

Wo ist der Speisesaal?
Where's the dining room?

Wann gibt es Frühstück?
What time is breakfast?

Ich bin um ... Uhr wieder da
I'll be back at ... o'clock

Ich reise morgen ab
I'm leaving tomorrow

Essen und Trinken
• eating and drinking

Zum Wohl!
Cheers!

Es ist köstlich/ scheußlich
It's delicious/awful

Ich trinke/rauche nicht
I don't drink/smoke

Ich esse kein Fleisch
I don't eat meat

Nichts mehr, danke
No more for me, thank you

Könnte ich noch etwas mehr haben?
May I have some more?

Wir möchten bitte zahlen
Bill/check, please

Ich hätte gerne eine Quittung
Can I have a receipt?

Nichtraucherbereich
No-smoking area

die Gusundheit
• health

Ich fühle mich nicht wohl
I don't feel well

Mir ist schlecht
I feel sick

Können Sie einen Arzt holen?
Can you get me a doctor?

Wird er/sie sich wieder erholen?
Will he/she be all right?

Es tut hier weh
It hurts here

Ich habe Fieber
I have a fever

Ich bin im ... Monat schwanger
I'm ... months pregnant

Ich brauche ein Rezept für ...
I need a prescription for ...

Ich nehme normalerweise ...
I normally take ...

Ich bin allergisch gegen ...
I'm allergic to ...

deutsches register • German index

deutsch

A

à la carte 152
Aal *m* 294
Abdeckband *n* 83
Abdecktuch *n* 83
Abend *m* 305
Abenddämmerung *f* 305
Abendessen *n* 64
Abendkleid *n* 34
Abendmenü *n* 152
Abenteuerfilm *m* 255
Abfahrtslauf *m* 247
Abfalleimer *m* 61
Abfallentsorgung *f* 61
Abfallsortiereinheit *f* 61
Abfertigungsschalter *m* 213
Abflug *m* 213
Abflughalle *f* 213
Abfluss *m* 61, 72
Abflussrohr *n* 61
Abführmittel *n* 109
abheben 99
Abhebungsformular *m* 96
Abkühlgitter *n* 69
Ablage für Ausgänge *f* 172
Ablage für Eingänge *f* 172
Ablasshahn *m* 61
Ableger *m* 91
Abmessungen *f* 165
Absatz *m* 37
Abschlag *m* 232
abschleppen 195
Abschleppwagen *m* 203
Abschnitt *m* 96
Abschürfung *f* 46
Abschuss *m* 281
Abschussrampe *f* 281
Abseilen *n* 248
Abseits *n* 223
abseits der Piste 247
Absender *m* 98
Absperrhahn *m* 61
Abspielen *n* 269
Abteil *n* 209
Abteilungen *f* 49
Abtropfbrett *n* 67
Abzeichen *n* 189
abziehen 82
Abzug *m* 271
Accessoires *n* 36
Achat *m* 289
Achillessehne *f* 16
Achse *f* 205
Achselhöhle *f* 13
acht 308
Achteck *n* 164
achter 309
Achterdeck *n* 214
achthundert 308

achtzehn 308
achtzehnter 309
achtzig 308
achtzigster 309
Ackerbaubetrieb *m* 183
Ackerland *n* 182
Acrylfarbe *f* 274
Adamsapfel *m* 19
addieren 165
Adler *m* 292
Adresse *f* 98
Adzukibohnen *f* 131
Aerobic *n* 251
Affe *m* 291
Afghanistan 318
Afrika 317
After-Sun-Lotion *f* 108
Ägypten 317
Ahorn *m* 296
Ahornsirup *m* 134
Aikido *n* 236
Airbag *m* 201
akademische Grad *m* 169
Akazie *f* 110
Aktenordner *m* 173
Aktenschrank *m* 172
Aktentasche *f* 37
Aktien *f* 97
Aktienpreis *m* 97
Aktionen *f* 227, 229, 233
Aktivitäten *f* 162, 245, 263
Aktivitäten im Freien *f* 262
Akupressur *f* 55
Akupunktur *f* 55
Alarmanlage *f* 58
Alaska 314
Albanien 316
Algerien 317
alkoholfreie Getränk *n* 154
alkoholfreien Getränke *n* 144
alkoholischen Getränke *n* 145
Allee *f* 299
Allergie *f* 44
Alligator *m* 293
Allzweckraum *m* 76
Alpenpflanze *f* 87
alpine Kombination *f* 247
als Fänger spielen 229
alt 321
Alternativtherapien *f* 54
Aluminium *n* 289
Amazonien 312
ambulante Patient *m* 48
Ameise *f* 295
Amethyst *m* 288
Amniozentese *f* 52
Ampère *n* 60

Amphibien *f* 294
an Bord gehen 217
an, bei 320
Ananas *f* 128
Ananassaft *m* 149
Anästhesist *m* 48
Anbau *m* 58
anbeißen 245
anbraten 67
anbringen 82
Anden 312
Andenken *n* 260
andere Geschäfte *n* 114
andere Kunstfertigkeiten *f* 275
andere Schiffe *n* 215
andere Sportarten *f* 248
Andorra 316
Anfang *m* 321
Angebot *n* 174
Angebote *n* 106
Angeklagte *m* 180, 181
Angelgeräte *n* 245
Angelhaken *m* 244
Angelrute *f* 244
Angelschein *m* 245
Angelsport *m* 244
angemacht 159
angereicherte Mehl *n* 139
Angler *m* 244
Angola 317
angreifen 220, 223
Angriff *m* 220, 237
Angriffszone *f* 224
Anhang *m* 177
Anhänger *m* 36, 266
Anker *m* 214, 240
Ankerwinde *f* 214
Anklage *f* 94, 180
Ankunft *f* 213
anlegen 217
Anorak *m* 31, 33
Anprobe *f* 104
Anreden *f* 23
Anrufbeantworter *m* 99
Anspielkreis *m* 224
anstreichen 83
Antifalten- 41
Antigua und Barbuda 314
Antiquitätenladen *m* 114
Antiseptikum *n* 47
Antwort *f* 163
antworten 163
Anwaltsbüro *n* 180
Anwendung *f* 176
Anzeigetafel *f* 104, 225
Aperitif *m* 153
Apfel *m* 126
Apfelsaft *m* 149
Apfelstecher *m* 68
Apfelwein *m* 145

Apfelweinessig *m* 135
Apotheke *f* 108
Apotheker *m* 108
Apothekerin *f* 189
Apparat *m* 99
applaudieren 255
Aprikose *f* 126
April *m* 306
Aquamarin *m* 288
Aquarellfarbe *f* 274
Äquator *m* 283
Äquatorialguinea 317
Arabische Meer *n* 313
Arbeit *f* 172
Arbeitgeberin *f* 24
Arbeitnehmer *m* 24
Arbeitsessen *n* 175
Arbeitsfläche *f* 66
Arbeitszimmer *n* 63
Architekt *m* 190
architektonische Garten *m* 84
Architektur *f* 300
Architrav *m* 301
Argentinien 315
Arithmetik *f* 165
Arm *m* 13
Armaturen *f* 201
Armaturenbrett *n* 201
Armband *n* 36
Ärmel *m* 34
ärmellos 34
Armenien 318
Armlehne *f* 210
Armstütze *f* 200
Aromatherapie *f* 55
aromatisch 130
aromatische Öl *m* 134
Art-déco- 301
Arterie *f* 19
Artischocke *f* 124
Arzt *m* 45, 189
Aschbecher *m* 150
Asche *f* 283
Aserbaidschan 318
Asien 318
Asphalt *m* 187
Ass *n* 230, 273
Assistentin *f* 24
assistierte Entbindung *f* 53
Ast *m* 296
Asteroid *m* 280
Asthma *n* 44
Astigmatismus *m* 51
Astronaut *m* 281
Astronomie *f* 281
Atemloch *n* 290
ätherischen Öle *m* 55
Äthiopien 317
Atlantische Ozean *m* 312
Atmosphäre *f* 282, 286

Atmung *f* 47
Atmungssystem *n* 19
Atrium *n* 104
Aubergine *f* 125
auf 320
auf der Stelle joggen 251
aufgehen 139
aufgenommen 48
aufgeregt 25
Aufhängung *f* 203, 205
aufkreuzen 241
Auflaufform *f* 69
Auflaufförmchen *n* 69
auflockern 91
Auflösungszeichen *n* 256
Aufnahme *f* 269
Aufsatz *m* 163, 233
Aufschlag *m* 231
aufschlagen 231
Aufschlaglinie *f* 230
aufstehen 71
auftauen 67
auftrennen 277
aufwachen 71
aufwärmen 154
Auge *n* 14, 51
Augenbraue *f* 14, 51
Augenbrauenstift *m* 40
Augenoptiker *m* 51
August *m* 306
aus 225, 226, 228, 320
aus Freilandhaltung 118
ausblasen 141
ausbrechen 283
Ausfahrt *f* 194
Ausfall *m* 251
Ausgang *m* 210
Ausgehen *n* 75
Auskunft *f* 99, 168
Auskunft *f* 99
ausländische Währung *f* 97
Auslandsflug *m* 212
Auslass *m* 61
auslaufen 217
Ausleger *m* 95
Auslegerkorb *m* 95
Ausleihe *f* 168
Ausleihe *f* 168
ausleihen 168
Auslöser *m* 270
Auspuff *m* 203
Auspuffrohr *n* 204
Auspufftopf *m* 203
ausrollen 67
Ausrüstung *f* 165, 233, 238
Aussage *f* 180
Ausschnitt *m* 34
Außenbordmotor *m* 215
Außenfeld *n* 229
Außentür *f* 59
Äussere *n* 198

deutsch

deutsch

deutsch

deutsch

deutsch

deutsch

deutsch

deutsch

englisches Register • English index

english

english

english

english

english

english

english

english

english

english

english

english

english

english

english

Dank • acknowledgments

DORLING KINDERSLEY would like to thank Tracey Miles and Christine Lacey for design assistance, Georgina Garner for editorial and administrative help, Sonia Gavira, Polly Boyd, and Cathy Meeus for editorial help, and Claire Bowers for compiling the DK picture credits.

The publisher would like to thank the following for their kind permission to reproduce their photographs:
Abbreviations key:
t = top, b = bottom, r = right, l = left, c = centre

Abode: 62; **Action Plus:** 224bc; **alamy.com:** 154t; A.T. Willett 287bcl; Michael Foyle 184bl; Stock Connection 287bcr; **Allsport/Getty Images:** 238cl; Alvey and Towers: 209 acr, 215bcl, 215bcr, 241cr; **Peter Anderson:** 188cbr, 271br. **Anthony Blake Photo Library:** Charlie Stebbings 114cl; John Sims 114tcl; **Andyalte:** 98tl; **apple mac computers:** 268tcr; **Arcaid:** John Edward Linden 301bl; Martine Hamilton Knight, Architects: Chapman Taylor Partners, 213cl; Richard Bryant 301br; **Argos:** 41tcl, 66cbl, 66cl, 66bl, 66cbl, 69cl, 70bcl, 71t, 77tl, 269tcc, 270tl; **Axiom:** Eitan Simanor 105bcr; Ian Cumming 104; Vicki Couchman 148cr; **Beken Of Cowes Ltd:** 215cbc; **Bosch:** 76tcr, 76tc, 76tcl; **Camera Press:** 27c, 38tr, 256t, 257cr; Barry J. Holmes 148tr; Jane Hanger 159cr; Mary Germanou 259bc; **Corbis:** 78b; Anna Clopet 247tr; Bettmann 181tl, 181tr; Bo Zauders 156t; Bob Rowan 152bl; Bob Winsett 247cbl; Brian Bailey 247br; Carl and Ann Purcell 162l; Chris Rainer 247ctl; ChromoSohm Inc. 179tr; Craig Aurness 215bl; David H.Wells 249cbr; Dennis Marsico 274bl; Dimitri Lundt 236bc; Duomo 211tl; Gail Mooney 277ctcr; George Lepp 248c; Gunter Marx 248cr; Jack Fields 210b; Jack Hollingsworth 231bl; Jacqui Hurst 277cfr; James L. Amos 247bl, 191ctr, 220bcr; Jan Butchofsky 277cbc; Johnathan Blair 243cr; Jon Feingersh 153tr; Jose F. Poblete 191br; Jose Luis Pelaez.Inc 153tc, 175tl; Karl Weatherly 220bl, 247tcr; Kelly Mooney Photography 259tl; Kevin Fleming 249bc; Kevin R. Morris 105tcr, 243tl, 243tc; Kim Sayer 249tcr; Lynn Goldsmith 258t; Macduff Everton 231bcl; Mark Gibson 249bl; Mark L. Stephenson 249tcl; Michael Pole 115tr; Michael S. Yamashita 247cctcl; Mike King 247cbl; Neil Rabinowitz 214br; Owen Franken 112t; Pablo Corral 115bc; Paul A.

Sounders 169br, 249ctcl; Paul J. Sutton 224c, 224br; Peter Turnley 105tcr; Phil Schermeister 227b, 248tr; R. W Jones 309; R.W. Jones 175tr; Richard Hutchings 168b; Rick Doyle 241cctr; Robert Holmes 97br, 277ctc; Roger Ressmeyer 169tr; Russ Schleipman 229; Steve Raymer 168cr; The Purcell Team 211ctr; Tim Wright 178; Vince Streano 194t; Wally McNamee 220br, 220bcl, 224bl; Yann Arhus-Bertrand 249tl; **Demetrio Carrasco / Dorling Kindersley (c) Herge / Les Editions Casterman:** 112ccl; **Dixons:** 270cl, 270cr, 270bl, 270bcl, 270bcr, 270ccr; **Education Photos:** John Walmsley 26tl; **Empics Ltd:** Adam Day 236br; Andy Heading 243c; Steve White 249cbc; **Getty Images:** 48bcl, 100t, 114bcr, 154bl, 287tr; 94tr; **Dennis Gilbert:** 106tc; **Hulsta:** 70t; **Ideal Standard Ltd:** 72r; **The Image Bank/Getty Images:** 58; **Impact Photos:** Eliza Armstrong 115cr; John Arthur 190tl; Philip Achache 246t; **The Interior Archive:** Henry Wilson, Alfie's Market 114bl; Luke White, Architect: David Mikhail, 59tl; Simon Upton, Architect: Phillippe Starck, St Martins Lane Hotel 100bcr, 100br; **Jason Hawkes Aerial Photography:** 216t; **Dan Johnson:** 26cbl, 35r; **Kos Pictures Source:** 215cbl, 240tc, 240tcr; David Williams 216b; **Lebrecht Collection:** Kate Mount 169bc; **MP Visual.com:** Mark Swallow 202t; **NASA:** 280cr, 280ccl, 281tl; **P&O Princess Cruises:** 214bl; **P A Photos:** 181br; **The Photographers' Library:** 186bl, 186bc, 186t; **Plain and Simple Kitchens:** 66t; **Powerstock Photolibrary:** 169tl, 256t, 287tc; **Rail Images:** 208c, 208 cbl, 209br; **Red Consultancy:** Odeon cinemas 257br; **Redferns:** 259br; Nigel Crane 259c; **Rex Features:** 106br, 259tc, 259tr, 259bl, 280b; Charles Ommaney 114tcr; J.F.F Whitehead 243cl; Patrick Barth 101tl; Patrick Frilet 189cbl; Scott Wiseman 287bl; **Royalty Free Images:** Getty Images/Eyewire 154bl; **Science & Society Picture Library:** Science Museum 202b; **Skyscan:** 168t, 182c, 298; Quick UK Ltd 212; **Sony:** 268bc; **Robert Streeter:** 154br; **Neil Sutherland:** 82tr, 83tl, 90t. 118, 188cctr, 196tl, 196tr, 299cl, 299bl; **The Travel Library:** Stuart Black 264t; **Travelex:** 97cl; **Vauxhall:** Technik 198t, 199tl, 199tr, 199cl, 199cr, 199ctcl, 199cctr, 199tcl, 199tcr, 200; **View Pictures:** Dennis Gilbert, Architects: ACDP Consulting, 106t; Dennis Gilbert,

Chris Wilkinson Architects, 209tr; Peter Cook, Architects: Nicholas Crimshaw and partners, 208t; **Betty Walton:** 185br; **Colin Walton:** 2, 4, 7, 9, 10, 28, 42, 56, 92, 95c, 99tl, 99tcl, 102, 116, 120t, 138t, 146, 150t, 160, 170, 191ctl, 192, 218, 252, 260br, 260l, 261tr, 261c, 261cr, 271cbl, 271cbr, 271ctl, 278, 287br, 302, 401.

DK PICTURE LIBRARY:
Akhil Bahkshi; Patrick Baldwin; Geoff Brightling; British Museum; John Bulmer; Andrew Butler; Joe Cornish; Brian Cosgrove; Andy Crawford and Kit Hougton; Philip Dowell; Alistair Duncan; Gables; Bob Gathany; Norman Hollands; Kew Gardens; Peter James Kindersley; Vladimir Kozlik; Sam Lloyd; London Northern Bus Company Ltd; Tracy Morgan; David Murray and Jules Selmes; Musée Vivant du Cheval, France; Museum of Broadcast Communications; Museum of Natural History; NASA; National History Museum; Norfolk Rural Life Museum; Stephen Oliver; RNLI; Royal Ballet School; Guy Ryecart; Science Museum; Neil Setchfield; Ross Simms and the Winchcombe Folk Police Museum; Singapore Symphony Orchestra; Smart Museum of Art; Tony Souter; Erik Svensson and Jeppe Wikstrom; Sam Tree of Keygrove Marketing Ltd; Barrie Watts; Alan Williams; Jerry Young.

Additional Photography by Colin Walton.

Colin Walton would like to thank:
A&A News, Uckfield; Abbey Music, Tunbridge Wells; Arena Mens Clothing, Tunbridge Wells; Burrells of Tunbridge Wells; Gary at Di Marco's; Jeremy's Home Store, Tunbridge Wells; Noakes of Tunbridge Wells; Ottakar's, Tunbridge Wells; Selby's of Uckfield; Sevenoaks Sound and Vision; Westfield, Royal Victoria Place, Tunbridge Wells.

All other images are Dorling Kindersley copyright. For further information see www.dkimages.com